That's Where I Live®

A Guide To Good Relationships

Christopher J. Godfrey, J.D.

Rick & Karen

Thanks for all
you do for life

Ch

Life Athletes Press

Nihil Obstat: Francis J. McAree, S.T.D.
                   Censor Librorum

Imprimatur: + Patrick J. Sheridan, D.D.
                   Vicar General
                   Archdiocese of New York

Written by Christopher J. Godfrey, J.D.
© 1999, Life Athletes, Inc.
All rights reserved
Printed in the United States of America
ISBN: 0-9676435-0-3
Photo credit: Compass Arts

Dedication

To Robert and Carol who, among other things, gave me eight brothers and sisters, and most especially to my wife Daria, who together with our children Alexandra, Catherine, Mary Grace, Anastassia, and John make me a better person.

Acknowledgements

Special thanks to the Knights of Columbus, Wellington Mara and Michael Pascucci for making this initiative a reality. I would also like to thank Sr. Marie Pappas, C.R. for being such an encouragement, and serving as my curricular guardian angel throughout this long process. I am also grateful to Dr. Catherine Hickey, Sr. Winifred Lyons, S.C., Fr. John Bonnici and their wonderful staffs for this opportunity. Thanks to Charles, Mary and Ellen Rice, Gene Quirini, Sr. John Dominic, Carol Puccio, Sr. Mary Doolittle, S.V., Fred and Lisa Everett, David Thomas and Fr. Michael Heinz, for reading this manuscript and providing welcome observations on improving its contents. Additional gratitude is due to Gene Quirini for his wonderful layout and design work. Thanks to Gerard Gallagher, Esq. for putting everything in legal order. And lastly, I would like to acknowledge my many teachers who are responsible for anything of value in this curriculum. Although you may have had doubts, your efforts were not entirely in vain.

About the Author

Chris Godfrey is the president of Life Athletes, and a member of the Indiana Bar. Prior to graduating from the University of Notre Dame Law School, he played nine years of professional football. As the right guard for the Super Bowl XXI champion New York Giants, he earned honors as All-Pro NFL Films, and All-NFC (AP, UPI). He was also a member of three University of Michigan Rose Bowl teams. Chris resides in South Bend, Indiana with his wife Daria and their five children.

Table of Contents

---

*Two class periods are devoted to this material, thereby allowing an opportunity to begin work on suggested projects.

CHAPTER 1

Where Do You Live?

We are what we love

When we meet people for the first time, we almost always ask them where they live. Why do we do this? Do we think that knowing where a person's mail is delivered helps us to know him or her any better? Not really. While it might make for polite conversation, it doesn't really tell us much about him. To *really* know where a person lives is to know what is in his heart. It is to know what he loves, and to know what he thinks is important.

Everyone wants to be happy

Have you ever slowed down long enough to ask yourself where *you* live? Have you ever asked: "Who am I," "Where am I going," or "What's really important?" These are not questions crazy people ask themselves. No, these are questions wise people have always asked themselves. We are all alike in this regard. It is how we are made.

We are also alike in that we all want to be happy. Generally speaking, happiness is getting what we want. However, we know from experience that this is not always true. Getting what we want does *not* always make us happy. The reason is that we sometimes want the wrong things, or are mistaken about the happiness to be found in them.[1]

Levels of happiness

To illustrate the relationship between our choices and our happiness, it useful to compare our choices with the quality of happiness they give us. The lowest level of happiness occurs when we maximize our pleasure and minimize our pain in order to achieve an instant gratification that passes almost as quickly as it comes. The next highest level occurs when we gain an advantage over others; this is a self-centered approach that yields short-term happiness. The next level chooses good simply because it is good, which is a way of being other-centered; doing this yields long-term happiness.

Finally, the highest level occurs when we choose and enjoy a relationship with God, which yields the greatest happiness of all. This is true because God is the supreme good. Since he alone is perfect, he alone can give perfect happiness. Moreover, since we came from him, we are returning to him. It makes sense therefore, that our highest happiness and fulfillment would come from our highest or ultimate end.

Do good and avoid evil
The knowledge that we should do good and avoid evil is something that we are all born with; it comes naturally to us. It helps us, because doing the good always leads to happiness in the long run. St. Thomas Aquinas, who is known for his exceptional wisdom, emphasized this when he said, "Happiness is the reward of virtue."[2] We will talk more about virtue later on, but for now let us just say that virtue means doing good.

You may ask then, "Why do we choose evil?" Good question. Part of the answer is that it is a mystery, which means we are incapable of fully understanding it and that God has to reveal it for us to know it. Other reasons are more obvious.

Apparent goods
Sometimes we are mistaken about what is good because things are not always what they appear to be. Things that appear to be good when they are not are called "apparent goods." These are not true goods, and they fool a lot of people. That's why we owe it to ourselves to be well informed. Simply to guess is not enough. We need good information if we are to make good decisions. Otherwise we will probably make bad ones – even if our intentions are good. This process of informing ourselves is called "forming our consciences."

Forming our consciences
To form our consciences correctly we need reliable sources of information that can help us to see the bigger picture. "A well-formed conscience is upright and truthful. It formulates its judgments according to reason, in conformity with the true good willed by the

wisdom of the Creator. Everyone must avail himself of the means to form his conscience" (*CCC* 1798).

We wouldn't drive at night without turning on our headlights, would we? The light helps us to know when to turn, when to stop, how fast we should go, etc. Without headlights we would see only shadows, and our passengers would also be very nervous. Making decisions on feelings alone is like driving without headlights; we won't see very much. We will talk more about reliable sources in the next chapter. But for now, remember that when we make choices between good and evil we need to be informed.

Ends justifying the means

Another reason for doing evil is hoping good things will come of it. Said another way, *how* we do something doesn't matter as long as it gets good results. This rationale is known as the "ends justify the means." However, when the means are evil, it is not only sinful, it is dangerous. History is filled with people justifying their bad behavior in this way. This kind of thinking creates more evil than we can imagine, and certainly more than we could ever control. Can you think of some examples?

What makes you happy?

Think for a moment of the things that make you happy. Go ahead and write them down - in no particular order. Just write them down as they occur to you. When you are finished, take a look at your list and note the similarities between the different items. Ask yourself how they are alike, and how they are different. If a stranger saw your list, what would he or she think of you? Would you be someone she would like to call friend? Why?

Real things last longest

It is "a no-brainer" to say that we benefit from making intelligent choices. This is especially true in our relationships with others. If we would take the time to think about them, we would have a better chance of having good ones. From experience we know that some things make us happier than others. We also know that the longer something lasts, the more real it is. Have you ever been a little sad even while you were having a good time? Perhaps the reason for your sadness was knowing that your happiness was eventually going to end. Everything in this life comes to an end. We don't want it to, but we know it is inevitable.

Think about your list of things that make you happy. List them according to their longevity, putting the ones that last the longest at the top. The ones at the top are more real because they are more substantial. If you had a choice between an item at the top and an item at the bottom, wouldn't you choose the one at the top? Sure you would, because the longer something lasts the happier you are. Wouldn't it be best to spend most of your time and energy on these things?

Perhaps you might consider adding some things to your life that are more permanent and thereby improve it. If you had the whole universe to choose from, what would you pick? The sun? The moon? The mess in your bedroom? Good guesses, but you are not even close. There is something that lasts even longer than these.

The excellence of love
The importance of good relationships has long been communicated to us through the arts. In fact, love has been a favorite topic of artists for centuries. Not just romantic love, but friendship and heroism too. Can you think of any songs or movies that speak of how love goes on? The permanence of love is something we know without even being told. Even so, God thought it was important enough to remind us of it. St. Paul tells us that Faith, Hope, and Love last forever, and that the greatest of these is love (1 Cor 13:13).

Love exists only within relationships. That is why good relationships are the key to our happiness. It is where we find love. If we want to be happy, we must have love. Love is more than sweet words, or a good time. It takes many forms within the many different kinds of relationships we have in our lives.

St. Paul gives us a pretty full description of it when he says: "Love is patient, love is kind. It is not jealous, [love] is not pompous, it is not inflated, it is not rude, it does not seek its own interests, it is not quick tempered, it does not brood over injury, it does not rejoice over wrongdoing but rejoices with the truth. It bears all things, believes all things, hopes all things, endures all things. Love never fails" (1Cor 13:4-8).

Questions

1. What is a conscience?

   The conscience is man's most secret core, and his sanctuary. There he is alone with God whose voice echoes in his depths (*CCC* 1795). Moral conscience, present at the heart of the person, enjoins him at the appropriate moment to do good and to avoid evil (*CCC* 1777, Rom 2:14-16).

2. What is a well-formed conscience?

   A well-formed conscience is upright and truthful. It formulates its judgments according to reason, in conformity with the true good willed by the wisdom of the Creator. Everyone must avail himself of the means to form his conscience (*CCC* 1798).

3. How should we form our conscience?

   The education of the conscience is a lifelong task. It is accomplished through prudent education that teaches virtue; it prevents or cures fears, selfishness and pride, resentment arising from guilt, and feelings of complacency, born of human weakness and faults. The education of conscience guarantees freedom and engenders peace of heart (*CCC* 1783).

4. What does the author mean by "That's where I live?"

   It is a statement of what we believe, of what we love, and of what we think is important.

5. Why is love desirable, and where do we find it?

   Love is desirable because it lasts forever, and it is found within relationships with other persons.

6. What is an apparent good?

   An apparent good is something that appears to be good when it is not.

7. What is "the ends justify the means"?

   The "ends justify the means" is a reason given for doing evil. The perpetrator commits an evil act in the hope that good will result. This is wrong.

Notes

[1] Thomas Aquinas, *Summa Theologiae*, I-II, 5, 8. For more on the nature of happiness, see preceding text starting with I-II, 3, 1.

[2] *Ibid.*, I-II, 4, 6; John 13:17.

CHAPTER 2

Can We Ever Know The Truth?

Right and wrong can be known, because the truth can be known
Asking ourselves questions like "Who am I," "Where am I going" or
"What's really important?" is useless unless we can know the truth
about things. What is the point in asking questions when there
aren't any answers? Since we are asking the questions, this must be
an indication that the truth does exist and that we can know it. We
need to know it. "Our lives can never be grounded upon doubt,
uncertainty or deceit. If we lived that way we would be threatened
constantly by fear and anxiety."[1] We want certainty. We don't want
propaganda, or opinions. We simply want to know how things really
are.

Faith and reason
The first thing to realize is that truth is truth. There are not different
truths. However, there are different ways in which we come to know
the one truth. These are called faith and reason. Simply said, faith is
adherence to truth revealed by God, while reason is adherence to
truth discovered by intellectual pursuit.

Some people think that the two are incompatible. They are wrong.
In fact, the two need each other. John Paul II begins his encyclical
Faith and Reason with this to say about them: "Faith and reason are
like two wings on which the human spirit rises to the contemplation
of the truth; and God has placed in the human heart a desire to
know the truth."

Without the help of faith, reason loses its direction, and without reason faith loses its ability to speak to everyone in every place.[2] For

15

example, without faith we can become so impressed with our technological advances that we forget that our original purpose was to improve people's lives – not make them worse. Similarly, without reason we can lose sight of the fact that religion is universal; what is true and unchangeable here is true and unchangeable everywhere. Without reason we become bogged down in feelings and personal experience. In summary, faith puts the work of reason into the proper context, while reason allows us to think about and understand what God has taught us.

Everyone is a believer
We also rely on belief to learn the truth. Not only in religion, but also in basic everyday things. To a greater or lesser extent we trust our parents, teachers, priests, sisters, scientists, news reports, etc. We simply do not have the time or the ability to conduct scientific investigations into every aspect of our physical world. We depend on trusted sources to teach us the truth about the unknown.

What are some of the things you trust in without testing them yourself? Have you ever flown in a plane without first studying the laws of aerodynamics? Have you ever walked across a street without getting the assurance of every motorist that he will stop when the light turns red? Make a list of all the things you do each day based on trusting another person's information.

God is a reliable source
As we go through life, faithfully forming our consciences and trying to choose good over evil, who do we turn to for reliable information? Who knows us best, and who wants us to have the best? Clearly, such a person should be considered a reliable source. Since God made us and loves us, he should be at the top of any thinking person's list.

While there are many things we can figure out on our own, there are some things that are so important to our happiness that God made a special effort to tell us about them. He sent Jesus to teach us, and the Holy Spirit to guide us. It is through the person of Jesus that he entrusted his Word to his Church. Today, God's Word comes to us in two forms: Sacred Scripture and Sacred Tradition. Sacred Scripture is the Bible, and Sacred Tradition is the teaching and example of Jesus given to the Apostles as well as what they learned from the Holy Spirit, and later passed on to us (*CCC* 80-87).

Faithful interpreters

How can we know what Jesus expects of us almost 2000 years after he ascended to heaven? Times change; how do we know what to do now? What is the Holy Spirit saying to us today? These are good questions. To interpret the Word of God, God has given us the Magisterium, which includes the bishops in communion with the Pope, the successor of the Apostle Peter. Together, under the leadership of the Pope they exercise their authority in the name of Jesus Christ, who entrusted this Deposit of Faith (Sacred Scripture and Sacred Tradition) to them, in order that they may faithfully preserve the truth for later generations. Again, some things are so important that God makes sure we have every chance to know them.

Sacred Scripture, Sacred Tradition and the Magisterium cannot survive without each other.[3] These three in agreement with each other give us the certainty of truth we seek. When we have questions regarding faith and morals, the Church is a reliable source, and worthy of belief.

Searching for the truth

While we are blessed to know the truth ourselves, we have a duty to respect others in their search for it. The best way to do this is by being a friend to them. Friends may not always agree with each other, but they always treat each other with respect and trust. However, mere "searching" is not enough. "Although each individual has a right to be respected in his own journey in search of truth, there exists a prior moral obligation, and a grave one at that, to seek the truth and to adhere to it once it is known."[4]

In other words, we have the right to search for the truth, but we also have a corresponding duty to live it when we find it. Life is not a game of searching for the sake of searching. It is childish to merely drift from experience to experience without any intention of seriously evaluating things or of holding on to the truth once we find it. It is like dribbling a basketball all over the court without any intention of scoring.

Our search for the truth is not an easy one because we all have limitations; our thinking isn't perfect, nor are our hearts perfect. It may sound funny, but sometimes we don't want to know the truth because it will require us to change. It is during times like these that we have to be smart enough and strong enough to do the right thing. Can you think of a time when doing the right thing was difficult? What did you give up, and what did you gain by doing the right thing?

Contradictions are never true

Hold on to your hats. We are going to talk about an idea that has needlessly confused generations of people. Some believe and teach that we cannot know anything for sure. The problem with this statement is that they are certain of it. How could they be? How can you be certain that you can never be certain? It is a contradiction to say such a thing, and contradictions are never true. This is called the principle of non-contradiction.

A contradiction is like talking out of both sides of our mouth at once. Coach Bill Parcells could never hold up a football and tell his team, "Gentlemen this is, and is not - a football." Either it is, or it isn't; it cannot be both at the same time. Similarly, one can not be certain and not-certain at the same time.

There is no freedom without truth

One last thing to remember: there are grave consequences when we deny the existence of absolute truths. To deny our ability to know the truth is to deny that existence has any meaning at all. It leads to a denial of our identity and humanity. If truth is rejected, then so is the notion of human dignity and our freedom. Truth and freedom work together. If we reject truth, we reject the only sure foundation of freedom. If truth can be changed so can our freedoms. In the next chapter we will discuss 4 truths or principles regarding human life that are the foundation of our freedom today.

Just as wrong reason and bad faith have led to great misery, right reason and faithfulness can lead us to happiness. "Happy the man who meditates on wisdom and reflects on knowledge"(Sir 14:20).

Questions

1. What is meant by the nature of a thing?
   Nature is defined as that which makes something what it is, as distinct from something else. It is the defining characteristics and behavior of a particular reality.

2. Are faith and reason incompatible?
   Faith and reason are not incompatible; they need each other.

3. Why is God a reliable source?
   God is a reliable source because he knows what is best for us and wants what is best for us.

4. How can we know the truth of God's will?
   We can know the truth of God's will with certainty when Sacred Scripture, Sacred Tradition, and the Magisterium are in agreement with each other.

5. What is the principle of non-contradiction?
   The principle of non-contradiction is that something cannot be and not-be at the same time under the same aspect.

6. Why is truth important to freedom?
   Our freedom is based upon the truth of human dignity. Without the truth, there is no human dignity. Without our dignity, we have no right to freedom.

Notes

[1] *Faith and Reason*, 26.
[2] *Ibid.*, 48.
[3] *Ibid.*, 55.
[4] *Splendor of the Truth*, 34.

CHAPTER 3

What Makes People So Special?

Human beings are different from the rest of creation
We are living at a time when there is near universal recognition of human rights. After many centuries of searching for the truth, we have discovered that there are rights inherent in every person. Inherent rights mean they exist whether or not anybody chooses to recognize them.

However there are many people and many organizations who do not "walk the talk." They make declarations about human rights while denying them in practice. They say one thing but do another. Why the contradiction? One reason is that they misunderstand the meaning of freedom. While they recognize freedom as an inherent human right, they fail to recognize that we are in this together; all people are children of God and therefore brothers and sisters. Even though we are individuals with hopes and dreams, we are also a people who share many of these same hopes and dreams.

We are social beings
When God asked Cain about Abel, Cain responded, "Am I my brother's keeper?" Pope John Paul II in his encyclical letter *Gospel of Life* comments: "Yes every man is his brother's keeper, because God entrusts us to one another. It is in view of this entrusting that God gives everyone freedom, a freedom which possesses an *inherently relational dimension*."[1] We are not simply unconnected individuals competing for limited natural resources, as some believe. Therefore any proclamation on human rights must be based on a proper understanding of people and their relationships.

The 4 Principles of Life

This chapter contains four principles about human life that will help you make informed decisions about people in the future. Since we will return to them in later chapters we will give them a name: The 4 Principles of Human Life. Pretty snappy, huh? The *Gospel of Life* inspires them.

Image of God

The first Principle of Human Life is that all human beings are made in the image of God (Gen 1:26-27, Ps 8:6). This makes us different from the rest of creation. It means we have an intellect, a will, and that we can know and love in a special way. Our intellects give us the ability to think, and our wills enable us to choose. Only people can do this. When was the last time your dog sat in a chair and read the newspaper? Or when was the last time your cat painted your portrait as you washed the dishes? It never happened. Animals don't think like that.

When was the last time your dog refused a table scrap because it was on a diet or fasting? It never happened. Dogs don't give a second thought to long-term consequences. If it feels good, they do it. Unlike animals we have the ability to discern and choose between what appears to be good, and what really is good. Our intellect helps us to know the difference.

In order to make good choices we must be well informed. This requires thought and study. Once we have discovered the truth, our wills must be strong enough to choose it. It does us no good to know the truth, but not act on it. Just as study strengthens our minds, making good choices in little things strengthens our wills to make good choices in big things. It is like weightlifting. Weightlifters start by lifting lighter weights until they are strong enough to handle the heavier ones.

But what really sets us apart from the plants and the animals is our ability to love in a giving sort of way. This "giving-love" is different from "taking-love." We love many things, but many of these "loves" are loved only for the pleasure they give us. For example, we may say we love both soccer and our parents. But the love we have for our parents is very different from the love we have for soccer. We may take pleasure from soccer, but the love we have for our parents involves more than just pleasure.

In fact, loving our parents may even involve a little pain and sacrifice. For example, obeying them can really be difficult sometimes. Nevertheless, doing so is an act of love. Similarly, the way to love God is to do what he asks of us. Jesus said, "If you love me you will obey my commandments" (Jn 14:15). In summary, giving ourselves to others in an appropriate way is the highest form of love, and it is one of the reasons human beings are so special.

Life is sacred

The second principle of the 4 Principles of Life is that human life is sacred (Jb 12:10, 1 Sm 2:6). Since we are different from the rest of creation, we should be treated differently from the rest of creation. We are not natural resources for others to use. To be sacred means to belong to God. We are the only part of creation that God has made for himself.[2] The *Catechism* teaches us that "Human life is sacred because from its beginning it involves the creative action of God and it remains forever in a special relationship with the Creator, who is its sole end" (*CCC* 2258).

Since we belong to God, it follows that we cannot belong to one another. That is why murder and slavery are wrong (Ex 20:13). We don't even belong to ourselves. The prohibition against suicide is not only a religious view, it is also a rational one. Since we did not give ourselves life, it follows that we cannot take it.[3]

For this reason, it is also wrong to use anybody. The Second Vatican Council said, "Whatever is opposed to life itself, such as any type of murder, genocide, abortion, euthanasia, or willful self-destruction, whatever violates the integrity of the human person, such as mutilation, torments inflicted on body or mind, attempts to coerce the will itself; whatever insults human dignity, subhuman living conditions, arbitrary imprisonment, deportation, slavery, prostitution, the selling of women and children; as well as disgraceful working conditions, where people are treated as mere instruments of gain rather than as free and responsible persons; all these things and others like them are infamies indeed. They poison human society, and they do more harm to those who practice them than to those who suffer from the injury. Moreover, they are a supreme dishonor to the *Creator*."[4]

Life is valuable

The third principle is that we are valuable. We may have a vague sense of this truth but let's ask the ultimate question: "Why?" Is it our looks, our athletic or academic ability? Are we valuable because we are popular, or are we valuable simply because we think we are? The answer is "no" to all of the above. Our value comes from God. His standard is the standard by which we are measured. Without God, we lose our dignity. That is why in cultures where the rights of God are denied, the rights of man are also denied.

God loves us so much that he gave us his only son Jesus to die a cruel death on our behalf (Jn 3:16). He did not do this for mankind in general, but for each one of us individually. He would have done this even if we were the only person who ever existed.

In the National Football League there is a saying among the players that "you are only as good as your last game." This means that you could be the hero of the game one week, and cut the next if you have a bad game. While this may be an exaggeration, it reflects a philosophy that is very popular today. It is called Utilitarianism. Utilitarians believe that people are only as valuable as their economic output. In other words, people who produce are valuable; everyone else is a drag on society. This would necessarily include the young, old, sick and infirm. Utilitarianism ultimately reduces human beings to objects of manipulation and exploitation.

Another popular philosophy teaches that pleasure increases the value of life while suffering decreases it. Some believe, and teach, that healthy animals are more valuable than sick human beings.[5] Fortunately our sufferings and deformities don't really decrease our worth. They may increase our pain, but they don't decrease our dignity as persons. Even in our sickness and pain we possess a spiritual and immortal soul with whom God desires to have an eternal relationship.

These are just two popular philosophies that can influence our thoughts about the value of human life. There are many more, and they are all around us. They are in our books, our entertainment, our workplaces and universities. The next time you are tempted to devalue the life of another, just look at a crucifix. If God is willing to be tortured and killed for people, don't you think we should value them too? Can you think of examples where people have been valued wrongly? Make a list of them, along with the value system used.

God has a plan

Our fourth and last principle is that God has a plan for our lives (Rom 8:29). We have a purpose and meaning. We are not just atoms in a vast chaotic cosmic soup driven by fate. No, the universe is ordered. The sun rises at a predictable time, one season follows another, and so on. We are not an accident. There is a reason why we are here, and there is work for us to do. He made us to know him, love him, and to serve him in this world and the next.

Do you recall the movie "It's a Wonderful Life," starring Jimmy Stewart? You will recall George Bailey tried to commit suicide because he was in despair and thought he was worth more dead than alive. He was so depressed that he wished he had never been born, because his life hadn't turned out as he had planned. He was "stuck" working at his father's savings and loan company that helped poor immigrant families buy homes. He did this instead of all the "exciting" things his friends were doing around the world.

An angel saved him from his suicide attempt and showed him what the town would have been like without him. After seeing all the friendships he missed, and how awful everyone's lives were without him, he changed his mind. All his good deeds, and all of his suffering and little sacrifices had an incredible impact on the life of the entire town.

It can be the same for each of us. No matter how bad things may seem to be, there is a reason for our being here. God has a plan for each one of us - even if we can't see it sometimes. He knows us personally. Jesus is the Good Shepherd who calls us each by name, and leads us to the path for which we are searching (Jn 10:3).

Everyone has a deep longing for meaning, and if that longing is frustrated it can lead to despair. Despair is prevalent because we don't know the principles of human life. Principles are helpful because they can be applied in any situation for good result. For example, in football you are likely to be successful if you hit somebody low and hard, and hit them again if they get up - even if you forgot the play! Similarly, "streamlining" as you swim helps you to go fast even if your strokes are imperfect.

These 4 Principles of Life apply to all situations. No matter how difficult the problem, if you apply these principles you will be in good shape. Without them, "our existence would be reduced to living in order to die."[6]

The Four Principles of Life

1. We are made in the image of God.
2. We are sacred.
3. We are valuable.
4. God has a plan for our lives.

Questions

1. What does it mean to be made in the image of God?
   To be made in the image of God means we have an intellect, a will, and that we can love in a giving, other-centered way.

2. Why is human life sacred?
   Human life is sacred because it belongs to God.

3. Why is human life valuable?
   Human Life is valuable because God values it enough to suffer and die for us.

4. Why did God create us?
   God created us to know him, love him, and to serve him in this life and the next.

5. Can the 4 Principles of Life be applied in any situation?
   The 4 Principles of Life can be applied in any situation, no matter how difficult. They are always true, and useful in making decisions regarding people.

Notes

[1] *Gospel of Life,* 19.
[2] *Guadium et Spes,* 24.
[3] See Plato, *Phaedo.*
[4] *Guadium et Spes,* 27.
[5] Prof. Peter Singer, *Practical Ethics* (1979), 97.
[6] John Paul II, Homily at St. Peter's Basilica, November 29, 1998.

CHAPTER 4

Our Relationship With God

The most important relationship we will ever have is the one we have with our Heavenly Father
God is love. Love is what God does full-time. He loves each of us fully, totally and completely. There is nothing that can separate us from God's love. There is nothing we can do to make him stop loving us. Moreover, his love is informed. He knows each of us fully, totally and completely, both the good and the bad. Most of all he knows our potential. He knows what we can be if we receive his gift of love and learn to love others.

Many of us are fortunate enough to experience love within our families, and later on from friends. But as we grow older we realize we need something more. We want a love that is deeper and more permanent. We want a relationship that will help us to know ourselves better, and fulfill us. A gnawing feeling tells us that there is something more in life, and that we are missing it. We want to reach our potential, and we don't know how to do it. St. Augustine recognized this when he prayed: "Our heart is restless until it rests in you."[1]

By nature, we long for something that only God can give us, something we cannot live without. Our lives are senseless to us if we don't encounter God's love. His love is a gift. We can't earn it no matter how good we act – it is free. Without a doubt, our most important relationship is the one we have with God. That is why our parents baptized and raised us in the Christian faith. They know that God is the source of all happiness. They also know that life is difficult, and they want us to get to heaven.

God is not a grandfather

Unfortunately, the faith of our parents cannot carry us indefinitely. We are our own persons. We need to develop our own relationship with our Heavenly Father. Our parents can't believe in him and love him for us. In the end, we are responsible for our own souls, and for living our baptismal commitment.

This is serious stuff, but God makes it easy for us. He wants to be our friend. He loves us just the way we are, and his greatest desire is for us to love him in return. That is why he made us: to know him, to love him and to serve him in this life and to be happy with him in the next.

Have you ever liked someone who ignored you? It hurts, doesn't it? This is not unlike the way we treat Jesus sometimes. It is not that we consciously reject him. Rather it is more often that we allow other things to crowd him off our "radar screen." After all it is easier to pay attention to things we can see, than to God who is invisible. This is especially true at a time in our lives when our horizons are broadening, and our opportunities increasing.

But new opportunities bring new pressures. We can become so consumed with our own thoughts and plans that we forget about God. Because he is so patient and reliable, we tend to make him wait the longest. We don't think of him until we need him. But friends who only speak to you when they want something are not very good friends, are they? In addition, we miss out on developing a deep relationship with the most interesting persons around – the Holy Trinity.

Think about the great characters of history and why they would be interesting to talk to. Perhaps their genius created a marvelous invention or a great object of art. Or maybe they performed a heroic act inspired by devoted love. All of these admirable qualities are found in God – only more so. The three persons of God know and love infinitely. All that we find admirable in others is found in the Holy Trinity. Moreover, unlike the great figures of history, the Father, Son and Holy Spirit are instantly accessible to us when we pray.

Tough love

What is it that causes us to grow up spiritually? Perhaps it is recognizing our need for God, and a desire to be his friend. This is a gift of grace that we must first accept. Often we resist, but God never gives up. And since we are all different, God deals with us in different ways. Chris Godfrey recounts how God used football to get his attention:

"Years ago I received a phone call telling me I was cut from the Green Bay Packers football team. It was my third cut from an NFL team in a year. Without even thinking about it, I fell to my knees and said, 'Lord I give up. Whatever you want me to do, wherever you want me to go – you're the boss now.'

"Even though I was Catholic, I had never prayed like that before. Sure I loved God when I was younger, went to Mass on Sunday, and even prayed at night sometimes. But as I grew older, I started to drift away from God without even realizing it. I wasn't a bad guy; I never hurt anyone on purpose. But little by little, I stopped looking to God. I developed a divided heart. I claimed to be a Christian, but it was really my views and desires that mattered most, not God's.

"Because of my divided heart I grew weaker, less confident, and less happy – especially when I asked myself those important questions: 'Who am I?,' 'Where am I going?,' 'What is really important?' Nevertheless, football remained an important part of my life. It was fun, and it provided me an opportunity to prove myself. I did well in college, and played on three Rose Bowl teams for the University of Michigan. Although I wasn't picked in the NFL draft, I was offered a free-agent contract with the Washington Redskins. Nobody really thought I would make the team, because it is very difficult to get a job playing professional football. You have to be both good and lucky.

"That summer I got in the best shape of my life. Training camps in the NFL are brutal experiences, and I had to be ready. Teams practice and meet from morning until night for many weeks. Players get hot, tired, injured and homesick. I was no exception, except that I had the additional anxiety of knowing I was a long shot in making the team. But by the end of camp my teammates and the media thought I was going to do it.

"During this time I made new friends and enjoyed many new experiences. I also enjoyed all the attention I received. Being a Redskin in Washington D.C. made me very popular. One night, while driving in a friend's moon-roof Mercedes, I looked out at the monuments and city lights, and decided to 'let go' and have as much 'fun' as possible that season.

"The next day I was cut. I was shocked. It was so unfair; I thought I had earned a spot on the team. My teammates were surprised too. Nevertheless, the next day I was back home in Detroit washing the family dishes and wondering what happened to my big plans. Even though it was unfair, it turned out to be one of the best things that ever happened to me.

"Two weeks later the New York Jets signed me, and I spent the year playing backup defensive lineman. Although I was back in another big city, I wasn't as cocky as before. The following year, I injured my knee the day before training camp. The Jets cut me a couple of weeks later. After the long fourteen-hour drive home, I found a note waiting for me from the Green Bay Packers. They wanted me in their training camp the next day.

"I decided to give football one more chance. After a week, I was told I made the team. I was excited, and my family brought my things out to me. The next day I was awakened by a phone call telling me I was cut – for the third time in a year. I just hung up the phone and fell to my knees. I had run out of plans. I no longer felt in control of my life. What more could I do?

"After I had checked out of my hotel, and cleaned out my locker at Lambeau Field, the Packer's Head Coach, Bart Starr, apologized for cutting me, and asked me to stay with the team. I was flabbergasted. I had been around long enough to know that mistakes like that just don't happen in the National Football League. I knew that, somehow, God had a hand in it. And because God was close to me, I wanted to get closer to him. I wanted to return his offer of friendship.

"A week later I was invited to the team's Bible Study. I decided to attend, because I was looking for ways to get closer to God. While I was at that study, the Bible seemed to come alive. Words I had seen and heard before took on a whole new significance. One passage in particular jumped out at me. It was Matthew 6:33, 'But seek first the kingdom [of God] and his righteousness and all these things will be given you besides.'

"To me that meant I had to get my priorities straight. I needed to do things God's way first, and then everything else would follow. I also realized that this passage is a promise God makes to each one of us. Even though things went badly for me at first, I held onto that promise. I separated my shoulder the next year in training camp and was again cut. Then the whole league went on strike, making it impossible for me to play with another team. I soon found myself back in Detroit looking for a job in the midst of a severe economic recession.

"Strangely, even though I was out of work and engaged to be married, it was really a good time for me spiritually. The lack of distractions gave me the opportunity to grow on the inside. I met others who taught me more about my faith. I gained a deeper understanding of the sacraments, and how they made Jesus present in a real way. It was like being on an extended retreat.

"However, it wasn't long before things got busy again. A new football league was formed, and I signed with the Michigan Panthers of the United States Football League. I changed positions from defense to offensive line, and became a starting left tackle. We won the USFL Championship that year. The next year I signed a contract with the New York Giants, and became their starting right guard. A couple of years later I made some All-Pro teams and we won Super Bowl XXI. I even got married and had a couple of children by that time.

"God keeps his word, and if you do things God's way everything will work out well. Even though having a Super Bowl ring is great, having an identity as God's son is even better. I am thankful for the difficulties that prompted me to put my life into God's hands. I spend much more time on our relationship than I ever did before."

Purity of heart
Chris admitted his need after getting cut three times in a year. His limitations and frustrations made him realize he needed something or someone else. Only Jesus Christ can give us meaning, and our true identity and mission in life. Without him our lives are senseless. Therefore, we must with all of our unrest, uncertainty, weakness and

sinfulness draw near to Christ.[2] Don't wait until you "feel" holy, because it is never going to happen.

Chris' problem was his divided heart. He tried to have it both ways. He tried to be God's friend and the world's friend at the same time. This is a contradiction, and a contradiction is never true. If the world is defined as a place or an attitude that refuses to honor God, then Chris could not be a friend of both at the same time. Chris loved God with words, but not with his heart. His faith became a religion of rules that burdened him, rather than something that enlivened him. It was not until he remembered Jesus as a living and knowable friend that his life got turned right side up again.

Jesus said, "Blessed are the pure in heart, for they shall see God" (Mt 5:8). "Pure in heart refers to those who have attuned their intellects and wills to the demands of God's holiness, chiefly in three areas: charity; chastity or sexual rectitude; love of truth and orthodoxy of faith. There is a connection between purity of heart, of body, and of faith…." Purity of heart "enables us to see according to God, to accept others as 'neighbors'; it lets us perceive the human body – ours and our neighbor's – as a temple of the Holy Spirit, a manifestation of divine beauty (*CCC* 2518-2519)."

Purity of heart is to will one thing. It means being focused. It is a source of strength. Jesus acknowledged its importance to our spiritual lives when he taught, "You shall love the Lord your God with all your heart, with all your soul, and with all your mind. This is the greatest commandment and the first commandment. The second is like it: You shall love your neighbor as yourself" (Mt 22:37-39).

Pearl of great price
Jesus' relationship with us is as unique as each one of us is unique. With him we are never a number, never just another face in the crowd. Everyone has his or her own story, and every story is important.

The stories of the saints all point to the same thing. They treasure their relationship with Jesus; he is the pearl of great price (Mt 13:45-46). We may think of sainthood as something that does not happen to "real people." This is flat-out wrong. All of us have the opportunity to say "yes" to God many times a day. Sainthood isn't only achieved by dying a martyr's death. It can be achieved by loving others and doing our day-to-day work well for the love of God. The Holy Spirit is working in the hearts of millions of people, including our own. He is gentle, and does not force himself on anyone. If we let him, he will make us saints too.

Questions

1. What is the greatest relationship we can ever have? Why?

A relationship with our Heavenly Father is the best relationship we can ever have, because he is eternal and the source of all love. We are made to be in relationship with him. Without him we are incomplete and therefore we could never be happy.

2. How do we earn God's love?

Sorry, this is a trick question. We can never earn God's love. We already have it. There is nothing we can do to lose it. Any separation we experience from him is of our own choosing. He always waits for us to return with open arms.

3. Why do we need Jesus Christ?

Only Jesus can give us meaning, and our true identity and mission in life. Without him our lives are senseless.

4. Which is stronger: a pure heart or a divided heart? Why?

A pure heart is stronger, because if we are focused we are more likely to achieve our goal; in this case our goal is the "pearl of great price" (Matt 13:45-46).

5. Who is a reliable source for forming your conscience?

God is a reliable source. When forming our consciences we should always look to him first. He is the only one who is all-wise and all-loving. That means he knows what is best for us, and he wants what is best for us. Of all the advice being offered us, we should always listen for God's, because his is the most trustworthy.

Notes

[1] St. Augustine, *Confessions,* I, 1.
[2] *Redemptor Hominis,* 10.

CHAPTER 5

Our Relationship With Others

Good relationships are the key to our happiness
In Chapter 1 we discussed some questions that wise people have always asked themselves. Do you remember them? Even though these people may have lived a long time ago, we can still benefit from their discoveries. This is because we enjoy the same human nature they did. Technology changes, but the "wiring" inside human beings remains the same. If we make the effort to understand our ancestors, they can help us in our own search for happiness.

One of the things our wise ancestors discovered is that our relationships have a profound impact on us. It is through them that we give and receive love. And since we have different kinds of relationships, there are different ways of expressing this love. Depending on the type of relationship, some expressions of love are more appropriate than others. For example, holding a door open and saying "Good morning!" may be an appropriate expression of love for a stranger, whereas the hug and kiss you normally give your parents would not be.

Determining what is an appropriate expression of love isn't always easy. That is why we need reliable sources of information to help us decide. As we discussed, God is a reliable source. We will talk more about knowing God's will later on. For now, remember that sometimes an entire generation can forget the principles of good relationships, and cause their children a great deal of suffering. But younger generations can rediscover these truths and revitalize the world with the understanding that good relationships are the key to our happiness.

Our moral environment
Once again we are realizing that our actions affect those around us. We already know how this principle applies to our physical environment. For example, if we pour dirty motor oil into the river we make the river dangerous for plants, fish, and other living things. We even make it dangerous for ourselves.

The same idea applies to our moral environment, which is more important because it impacts souls. Our bodies live only a short time, but our souls last for eternity. The pollution of a river is sad, but the pollution of a heart is tragic. Remember, the longer something lasts, the more real it is. Our souls are precious.

The good
Think about it. When you see someone do a good thing, like helping someone, don't you get a little inspired? Don't you want to do the same? Or at the very least aren't you glad that there are people in the world who do them? You appreciate it when somebody does something nice for you – don't you? And when somebody does, aren't you more inclined to do something nice for others? Sure you are; it puts you in a better mood. There are far more opportunities for improving our moral environment than for recycling cans and paper. Can you think of any?

The bad
Just as seeing good things inspires us, seeing bad things tempts us. When people present an attitude or a behavior that causes us to sin, they are guilty of committing scandal (Matt 18:6-9). For example, when we see people lie and cheat, we feel like saying: "What's the use – everyone else is doing it, why can't I?" This is especially true when we are in a position of leadership. Why do you think this is so? Can you think of any examples where leaders have affected their moral environments for good or evil? If we are given a choice, what should we look for in a leader? Why?

The powerful
The news media and entertainment industries are leaders in shaping public opinion. They reach a lot of people and they reach them often. The more we hear something the more we are inclined to believe it – even if it is wrong. Do you think the messages they are communicating are improving or polluting our moral environment?

Can you think of some examples? What should they do more often? What should they do less often? What should we do about our own choices of entertainment? Why?

Our reputation

We can also affect others through our reputations. For example, if we have a good reputation, people tend to think well of us as well as those closest to us. We do our families and friends good service when we earn a good reputation. We also give glory to God. On the other hand, a *bad* reputation can hurt them. This may be unfair and prejudicial, but people tend to protect themselves until they learn to trust you as an individual. The bad behavior of some can spoil the moral environment for all the others.

Remember our discussion about the most important things? Here is the advice wise King Solomon gave his son about the value of a good reputation: "A good name is more desirable than great riches, and high esteem, than gold and silver" (Prv 22:1). A good reputation is also long lasting: "The memory of the just will be blessed, but the name of the wicked will rot" (Prv 10:7). Can you think of some examples where your reputation could help or hurt yourself - and others? Make a list of all the people who would be affected if your reputation were to change from what it is today.

Getting good friends

We all want good friends. But in order to have good friends, we have to be a good friend. And in order to be a good friend we need to be a good person.[1] After all who wants a good friend who isn't a good person? By definition, a bad person cannot be a good friend, because friends care about friends. Friendship requires being "other-centered." It requires thinking of others as highly as ourselves. Being a good person means giving the best of ourselves to others. It means doing what is right no matter what situation we are in.

Most people are a mixture of the two. It is not uncommon for someone to act like our friend one day and not the next. People like this are very frustrating. That is why other-centered people make the best friends. They are more reliable. So if you want good friends, be a good friend by being other-centered.

Masters of our internal universe

You can develop other-centeredness through at least two approaches. First, you begin to reach out to others, and secondly you can also begin to deny yourself. In order to receive others, it helps to make room for them, doesn't it? If you invited someone to spend the night at your house wouldn't you clean up your guest room? That is what self-denial or mortification accomplishes. It makes room for others in our lives by being less self-centered.

Fasting is a good example of self-denial. By denying our body's craving for food we make room for others, namely God. We do this to establish control over our bodies, which are always craving some sort of pleasure or comfort. By fasting we are saying, "I control my body, my body does not control me." This kind of control is powerful. Can you think of any other ways to grow in this power?

No pain, no gain

Controlling their bodies in order to achieve great things is what athletes do all the time. Do you think they just show up for the game and play? No. They spend hours, months and years saying "no" to their bodies' craving for pleasure and ease. They eat foods that are good for them; they avoid foods that are bad. They choose to train instead of hanging out with their friends. They run and lift weights when they don't feel like it. They don't stay out late because they need their sleep. The list could go on and on. The point is that they set their goals high and then make the little sacrifices necessary to achieve them. A popular way of describing this self-denial is "no pain, no gain."

Self-denial gives us power to be other-centered by weakening our selfishness. It is difficult because self-centeredness comes naturally to us; our bodies always struggle against being other-centered. Nevertheless good relationships are worth the effort because they make us happiest. Can you think of a relationship in your life that needs a little work? Think of one thing you can do to improve that relationship. Do you care enough to do it? Jesus said, "Greater love has no one than this, that one lay down his life for his friends" (Jn 15:13).

Other-centeredness is not only good for others; it is also good for us. Remember the question we asked in Chapter 1: "Who am I?"

The Bible tells us how to find out: "Whoever seeks to keep his life shall lose it, and whoever loses his life shall preserve it" (Lk 17:33, *CCC* 1889). Building on this, the Church teaches us that "Man can fully discover his true self only in a sincere giving of himself." The answer to who we are as individuals can only be discovered by giving ourselves to others as Jesus did. Our best opportunities arise within our day-to-day relationships.

Questions

1. What is the key to our happiness?
   Good relationships are the key to our happiness.

2. What is meant by "moral environment?"
   Our moral environment is that part of our environment that affects our spiritual health. Just as our physical environment affects our physical health, our moral environment affects our spiritual health. The good and evil around us can either inspire us or tempt us.

3. Why are the media such an important element of our moral environment?
   The media have a powerful impact on our moral environment because they are so pervasive. They reach more people with their messages than any individual can. Moreover, they can present their messages in more compelling ways utilizing powerful audio/visual technology.

4. How do we get good friends?
   We get good friends by being good friends, and the way we become a good friend is by being a good person. A friend who is not a good person will not care enough for his friends, and care more about doing what he wants to do than in doing what is right.

5. Why is it important to be other-centered?
   It is important to be other-centered because it is the way we become good and happy people. "Man can fully discover his true self only in a sincere giving of himself" (*Guadium et Spes* 24).

Notes

[1] "Do to others whatever you would have them do to you"
(Matthew 7:12); "So be perfect, just as your heavenly Father is
perfect" (Matthew 5:48).

CHAPTER 6/7

People Are Created Within Relationships

Our Relationship with Ourselves and our Family

Since we have different kinds of relationships, it follows that we relate differently to different people. It only makes sense that a sign of affection within one relationship may not be appropriate in another. As we discussed, kissing and hugging a stranger is inappropriate, while kissing and hugging our parents is not. Virtue is the power to know what is appropriate under the circumstances. In these chapters we will take a look at our relationships by first considering our character, and then our relationship with our family.

The key ingredient

We need to remember that in order to get good friends, we need to be a good friend. And the way to be a good friend is to be a good person. What does it mean to be a good person? For our purposes we'll keep it simple by defining a good person as a virtuous person.

At an NFL coaches' convention a few years ago, coaches were asked the following question, "What makes for a good team?" Everyone laughed when a wise guy shouted out, "Good players!" Then, Chuck Noll, the Pittsburgh Steelers coach who had won more Super Bowls than any other coach, stood up. A hush fell over the room as everyone strained to hear what he had to say. He said simply, "Your good players need to be good people."[1]

It's been said that a chain is only as strong as its weakest link. No matter how strong the other links may be, a chain cannot bear more stress than its weakest link can bear. Once the weak link breaks, the entire chain breaks. Coach Noll knew that his teams would only be able to handle as much as his most talented players could handle. Winning championships requires not only talent, but heart as well. The trick is to get both of them in your players. This is harder than it sounds. If it were easy, teams would not waste millions of dollars a year on players who fail in the NFL.

There are accurate ways to measure a player's physical ability. We can time him in a 40-yard dash to test his speed, and have him lift weights to test his strength. But how do we measure his heart? Don't we all have a heart? Well, yes and no. We all have a blood-pumping heart, but the heart we are talking about here is character. It has both strengths and weaknesses. These are sometimes referred to as virtues and vices. Like the links of a chain, together they form one entity – our character. The *Catechism* defines virtue as "an habitual and firm disposition to do the good. It allows the person not only to perform good acts, but to give the best of himself" (1803). In short, virtue is the habit of doing good.

Can you see why the coach valued virtue? He knew that talent was worth very little unless a player used it in the right way. Of what value is a talented player if he doesn't direct his talents towards team goals? For example, if he won't study his play book, or if he is undisciplined and always getting penalized, he will hurt the team more than help it. What good is he to the team if he quits when things get difficult, or if he is quarrelsome in the locker room?

Because we are all born with different natural tendencies, some virtues come easier to us than others do. Virtues are things we need to work at if we want to acquire them. "These moral virtues are acquired by human effort. They are the fruit and seed of morally good acts" (*CCC* 1804).

Why would we make the effort to acquire virtue? The primary reason is that God wants us to. The *Catechism* says, "The goal of a virtuous life is to be like God" (1803). But as with everything else, God only asks us to do what is good for us. He knows it is the best way to be happy and to acquire good friends. It is the way we express giving, other-centered love, which is the characteristic of a human being.

A virtuous person is one who can direct his or her energies to a good end. "Human virtues are firm attitudes, stable dispositions, habitual perfections of intellect and will that govern our actions, order our passions, and guide our conduct according to reason and faith" (*CCC* 1804).

Our first training camp

The hardest part about athletics is the training required. Although it is difficult, it is necessary for a good performance. It also has the added benefit of helping us develop a balanced personality, which is necessary for a happy life. For this reason the Church has long valued sports and exercise when done in the right in proportion.[2] But before we can run we need to learn to walk, and that is where our families come in.

Like the farm system of professional baseball, the family is the place where we prepare for the "big leagues." It is a place where we learn to grow in virtue. Through the example and instruction of those who love us, we are able to grow in the power of self-giving.

Our families are really a great gift. We might not always think of them in this way, but it is true. They provide us a unique opportunity to learn how to give and receive love.

Just as we did not choose to be born, we did not choose our families. It is similar to being drafted in professional baseball. A player must report to the team that drafts him; he has no say in the matter. Even if he is a life-long Yankees fan, if the Red Sox draft him, he must go to Boston. This then becomes an opportunity for him to grow in any number of virtues, which he would have otherwise missed. Who knows? He may even learn to appreciate being a Red Sox.

The same can be said for our families. We can wish they were different or we can learn to enjoy them just as they are. Even though our families can be a source of irritation at times, we should pause and wonder over these mysterious bonds. They are really a great blessing. We may soon realize that God places us in families because he loves us. And even if they are imperfect, good can still come of it.

What is a family?
Unfortunately we have gotten in the habit of calling most any
happy group or community "family." While this may add substance
to the group, it does so at the expense of true families. It can make
families seem commonplace when in fact they are really quite
extraordinary.

A family is a community which is established upon the consent of
the spouses. It is a man and a woman united in marriage, together
with their children. This should be considered the normal reference
point by which the different forms of family relationships are evaluated.

"Marriage and the family are ordered to the good of the spouses
and to the procreation and education of children. The love of the
spouses and the begetting of children create among members of the
same family personal relationships and primordial responsibilities.
Its members are persons equal in dignity. Moreover, for the good of
its members and of society, the family necessarily has many responsibilities, rights, and duties" (*CCC* 2201-2203).

Our most important lesson
The foremost duty and privilege of parents is the education of their
children. Parents have a powerful influence on a child's relationship
with God. John Cardinal O'Connor shared one of his childhood
experiences as an example: "Does every kid have an older sister who
keeps telling him he's adopted? I sure did. She's the same one who
told me on a late Christmas Eve that Santa Claus was downstairs in
our kitchen with his whiskers caught in the gas range. That worried
me a great deal. That I had allegedly been left in a basket on the
front doorstep and taken into the family didn't worry me in the
slightest. On the contrary, it made me feel special. In fact, I couldn't
wait to tell my mother and father!

"I remember the day I did. My father looked me right in the eye
and put his hand on my little shoulder. His answer was as important to the rest of my life as anything I have ever heard since. 'This
is your mother, son, and I'm your father. You were born in the
house. But if we had found you in a basket on the doorstep, we
would have been proud to bring you in and love you as much as we
do now.' That's called security. I have always been grateful to my sister that she raised the question.

"There's a difference now. I no longer have to think little-boy thoughts about what to get my father for Father's Day. I always offer Mass for him, of course, which he liked most when I was a young priest before he died. But apart from that, I spend much of the day grateful for what he gave me; the trust I felt in him was the beginning of my trust in God. Of that, I am certain. I could always believe my father. He never told less than the truth."[3]

Mr. O'Connor probably had no idea that his words would impact so many souls. In his simple act of love and obedience, he formed not only his son but also everyone his son has ever touched, which is a considerable number given the size of his responsibilities as Cardinal Archbishop of New York. A similar truth is expressed in the adage "The hand that rocks the cradle rules the world." This eloquently explains a mother's influence in the world. Even though she may never enter public life herself, her children may. More than anything else parents impact the world through their children.

Indeed, the *Catechism* calls the family the "original cell of social life. It is the natural society in which husband and wife are called to give themselves in love and in the gift of life. Authority, stability, and a life of relationships within the family constitute the foundations for freedom, security, and fraternity within society. The family is the community in which, from childhood, one can learn moral values, begin to honor God, and make use of freedom. Family life is an initiation into the life of society" (*CCC* 2207).

The virtue of piety
As we have discussed, our growth in virtue is largely due to our family's influence. Piety is a virtue that helps us to understand and benefit from this relationship with our family. Piety is respect for God's design in creation, and the family is most certainly God's design for the human race.

"Piety is a profound respect for the forces that preceded us and brought us into being. It is reverence for God, nature, and parents. By means of piety, a person remains united with what is good in his past, what is valuable and helpful in his tradition."[4]

Piety is an antidote for the alienation so many people experience today. Through it we realize that we are connected, and that we do not stand alone. It gives us hope that our setbacks may serve to help those who come after us.

Grade
7

Piety ponders the important question, "Where have I come from?" Which helps us to answer the questions we asked in Chapter 1, "Who am I?" and "Where am I going?" Understanding God's plan for family life helps us to answer these important questions.

Questions

1. What is virtue?

   Virtue is an habitual and firm disposition to do the good.

2. What is the basic unit of society?

   The family is the basic unit of society.

3. What is a family?

   A man and a woman united in marriage, together with their children form a family.

4. What is the virtue of piety?

   Piety is respect for God's design in creation, and for the forces that preceded us and brought us into being. It is reverence for God, nature, and parents.

Notes

[1] Recounted by Coach Bill Parcells at New York Giants team meeting, 1985.

[2] For more on Church teaching regarding athletics see *A Catholic Perspective: Physical Exercise and Sports* by Robert Feeney.

[3] John Cardinal O'Connor, *On Being Catholic*, pp. 19-20.

[4] Donald DeMarco, *The Heart of Virtue*, p. 184.

CHAPTER 6/7

People Are Created Within Relationships

Our Relationship with the Church and the World

Beyond our personal concerns and our relationships with our families, we also have a relationship with the Church and the society at large. Along with these different relationships come different ways of relating. It is virtue that helps us to navigate through the complexities of this life and its relationships. The virtues give us the power to love others in an appropriate way under the circumstances.

The Church is a mystical reality, which means we don't always see and understand it completely. It is a reality of unfathomable proportions. Or as some would say, "It's awesome, dude." Words clearly fail us. That is why we use symbols, architecture, vestments, music, liturgy and the like to help us communicate these divine realities. Things that are true, beautiful and good are all reflections of God. The more something reflects God, the more it turns our thoughts toward him.

Communion of the saints

Baptism, along with all the other sacraments, binds us to Jesus and to one another (*CCC* 950). This is great news to people who are dispirited and alienated. Through baptism we become members of something bigger and better than anything the world has ever known. The Apostles Creed refers to this union as the Communion of Saints. "The communion of saints is the Church" (*CCC* 946). "But the most important member is Christ, since he is the head....Therefore, the riches of Christ are communicated to all the members, through the sacraments" (*CCC* 947).

Friendship with the saints
Our devotion to the saints should also be one of friendship whereby our bonds with them in the Holy Spirit are strengthened. "Exactly as Christian communion among our fellow pilgrims brings us closer to Christ, so our communion with the saints joins us to Christ....We worship Christ as God's Son; we love the martyrs as the Lord's disciples and imitators, and rightly so because of their matchless devotion towards their king and master. May we also be their companions and fellow disciples!" (*CCC* 957).

Do you have a devotion to a particular saint or saints? If you don't, ask God for inspiration. Take a moment and make a list of some of the saints you are familiar with. What virtues are they known for? Why do you think they might be helpful to us?

If you ever looked at a book of the saints, you will note that they are all very different from one another. They are not cookie-cutter copies of one another. This is because God made us all different, for different purposes. Do you remember the 4 Principles of Life? God has a plan for the talents he's given to each of us. It is up to us to say "yes" to that plan. The Blessed Virgin Mary is a great example. "By her complete adherence to the Father's will, to his Son's redemptive work, and to every prompting of the Holy Spirit, the Virgin Mary is the Church's model of faith and charity" (*CCC* 967).

One with Christ
The Church is one with Christ, and the saints are acutely aware of this unity. St. Augustine said, "Let us rejoice then and give thanks that we have become not only Christians, but Christ himself. Do you understand and grasp brethren, God's grace toward us? Marvel and rejoice: we have become Christ. For if he is the head, we are the members; he and we together are the whole man" (*CCC* 795).

Moreover, Pope St. Gregory the Great said, "Our redeemer has shown himself to be one person with the holy church whom he has taken to himself." Similarly St. Thomas Aquinas added, "Head and members form as it were one and the same mystical person." Finally, the *Catechism* recounts a reply given by St. Joan of Arc to her judges which sums it up nicely: "About Jesus Christ and the Church, I simply know they're just one thing, and we shouldn't complicate the matter" (*CCC* 795).

The Church as Bride

Jesus referred to himself as the "bridegroom," and the Church and its individual members as a bride betrothed to him.[1] St. Paul speaks beautifully of this betrothal when he says, "Christ loved the Church and gave himself up for her, that he might sanctify her."[2] It is interesting to note that St. Paul uses the marriage relationship between a man and a woman to describe the relationship between Christ and his Church.

This is not an exaggeration. Do you know that marriage is also modeled upon the relationship of the Holy Trinity?[3] It is true. The love between the husband and wife results in another person – their child. Similarly, the love between Father and Son is another person – the Holy Spirit.

That is why it is so important for both men and women to build their marriages upon a relationship with Jesus. He wants marriages to be happy and he is always present to help married couples overcome their inevitable difficulties. God has a plan for marriages, but we can only benefit from it if we are willing to follow him.

The world is our vineyard

We are now going to discuss our relationship with the world beyond our family and the Church. We all recognize in ourselves a need for a wider community wherein each of us contributes. For this reason we set up various forms of political communities, which exist for the good of all.

Pope John Paul II offers one of Jesus' parables as an illustration of our relationship with the world. "For the kingdom of heaven is like a householder who went out early in the morning to hire laborers for his vineyard. After agreeing with the laborers for a denarius a day, he sent them into his vineyard" (Mt 20:1-2).

This parable sets before our eyes the Lord's vast vineyard and the women and men who are called and sent forth by him to labor in it. The vineyard is the whole world, which is to be transformed according to the plan of God in view of the final coming of the Kingdom of God.[4]

"And going out about the third hour he saw others standing idle in the marketplace; and he said to them, 'You too go into the vineyard'

Grade
8

(Mt 20:3-4). From that distant day the call of the Lord Jesus 'You too go into my vineyard' never fails to resound in the course of history: it is addressed to every person who comes into this world."[5]

We are all a part of the team

When it comes to working in his vineyard, Our Lord did not make distinctions between religious and lay people wherein one group works, while the other watches. No, we are all in it together. Everyone in the Church has an active part to play in her mission and salvation. This is especially true today as we begin the Third Millennium. This great moment in history calls the lay faithful with particular urgency.[6]

Our dignity as Christians is the source of our motivation for working in the world. This status makes demands on us. Demands that are similar to the royal noblesse oblige where those of high rank have a duty to behave nobly towards others. More precisely, this dignity demands that we work in the Lord's vineyard: "Upon all the lay faithful, then, rests the exalted duty of working to assure that each day the divine plan of salvation is further extended to every person, of every era, in every part of the earth."[7]

Church and state

This mission does not necessarily conflict with our role as citizens of our country. Rather, in democracies such as the United States we have the opportunity to give substance to our political freedom by doing what ought to be done. "Democracy is not a substitute for morality....Its value stands-or falls-with the values which it embodies and promotes."[8] Our founders understood that freedom must be ordered towards higher things, if the country were to survive.

Even though our country's founders believed in the sovereignty of God, the United States is not a theocracy where political power and religious authority are combined. "The political community and the church are autonomous and independent of each other in their own fields. Nevertheless, both are devoted to the personal vocation of man, though under different titles."[9]

In other words, they both work towards the common good, but from different vantage points. The common good embraces all those conditions of social life by which individuals, families and organizations can achieve more thoroughly their own fulfillment. This has made the United States hospitable to many generations of different religious groups and non-believers who found a home here. The tolerance of our system of government is rooted in the Judeo-Christian principle that all human beings share the same rights, no matter what their religious, cultural, or physical differences.

The central issue
Our form of government was created very different from others. That is why it is referred to as an experiment. There was no guarantee that it was going to work. Since the United States is still very young (comparatively speaking), it is still too soon to tell if it will succeed. Nevertheless, it is interesting to note that both the Church and the state agreed that this experiment be built upon the unchanging truths of the human person.

Our Declaration of Independence states, "We hold these truths to be self-evident, that all men are created equal, that they are endowed by their Creator with certain unalienable Rights, that among these are Life, Liberty, and the Pursuit of Happiness." This assertion agrees with the basis of our work in the Lord's vineyard, which is to rediscover and make others rediscover the dignity of every human person.

"The dignity of the person is the most precious possession of an individual. As a result, the value of one person transcends all the material world. The words of Jesus, 'For what does it profit a man to gain the whole world and to forfeit his life?' contain an enlightening and stirring statement about the individual: value comes not from what a person 'has' – even if the person possessed the whole world! – as much as from what a person 'is': the goods of the world do not count as much as the goods of the person, the good which is the person individually."[10]

Grade
8

Questions

1. What is the Communion of Saints?
   The Communion of Saints is the Church, which shares the riches of Christ through the sacraments.

2. What is the significance of the parable of the householder and his vineyard?
   The vineyard is the world, which we are to transform according to the plan of God.

3. Are only those who have taken religious vows supposed to do God's work?
   No. Although the laity and religious have different types of work to do, they have all been called to participate in God's plan.

4. Are the Church and state opposed to each other?
   No. Although the Church and state are autonomous and independent of one another, they are alike in their concern for people, albeit from different vantage points.

Notes

[1] Mark 2:19, *CCC* 796; cf. Matthew 22:1-14; Matthew 25:1-13; 1 Corinthians 6:15-17; 2 Corinthians 11:2.
[2] Ephesians 5: 25-26, *CCC* 796.
[3] *Familiaris Consortio,* 11.
[4] *The Lay Members of Christ's Faithful People,* 1.
[5] *Ibid.,* 2.
[6] *Ibid.,* 3.
[7] Second Vatican Ecumenical Council, Dogmatic Constitution on the Church *Lumen Gentium,* 33.
[8] *Living the Gospel of Life: A Challenge to American Catholics,* A Statement from the U.S. Catholic Bishops, 25.
[9] Second Vatican Ecumenical Council, Pastoral Constitution on the Church in the Modern World *Gaudium et Spes,* 76.
[10] *The Lay Members of Christ's Faithful People,* 37.

CHAPTER 6/7

People Are Created Within Relationships

Our Relationship with Ourselves

At an NFL coaches' convention a few years ago, coaches were asked the following question, "What makes for a good team?" Everyone laughed when a wise guy shouted out, "Good players!" Then, Chuck Noll, the Pittsburgh Steelers coach who had won more Super Bowls than any other coach, stood up. A hush fell over the room as everyone strained to hear what he had to say. He said simply, "Your good players need to be good people."[1]

It's been said that a chain is only as strong as its weakest link. No matter how strong the other links may be, a chain cannot bear more stress than its weakest link can bear. Once the weak link breaks, the entire chain breaks. Coach Noll knew that his teams would only be able to handle as much as his most talented players could handle. Winning championships requires not only talent, but heart as well. The trick is to get both of them in your players. This is harder than it sounds. If it were easy, teams would not waste millions of dollars a year on players who fail in the NFL.

The Human Virtues

There are accurate ways to measure a player's physical ability. We can time him in a 40-yard dash to test his speed, and have him lift weights to test his strength. But how do we measure his heart? Don't we all have a heart? Well, yes and no. We all have a blood-pumping heart, but the heart we are talking about here is character. It has both strengths and weaknesses. These are sometimes referred to as virtues and vices. Like the links of a chain, together they form one entity – our character. The *Catechism* defines virtue as "an habitual and firm disposition to do the good. It allows the person not only to perform good acts, but to give the best of himself" (1803). In short, virtue is the habit of doing good.

Can you see why the coach valued virtue? He knew that talent was worth very little unless a player used it in the right way. Of what value is a talented player if he doesn't direct his talents towards team goals? For example, if he won't study his playbook, or if he is undisciplined and always getting penalized, he will hurt the team more than help it. What good is he to the team if he quits when things get difficult, or if he is quarrelsome in the locker room?

Because we are all born with different natural tendencies, some virtues come easier to us than others do, but not all. Virtues are things we need to work at if we want to acquire them. "These moral virtues are acquired by human effort. They are the fruit and seed of morally good acts" (*CCC* 1804).

Aside from getting noticed by an NFL coach, why would we make the effort to acquire virtue? The primary reason is that God wants us to. The *Catechism* says, "The goal of a virtuous life is to be like God" (1803). But as with everything else, God only asks us to do what is good for us. He knows it is the best way to be happy and to acquire good friends. It is the way we express giving, other-centered love, which is the characteristic of a human being.

A virtuous person is one who can direct his or her energies to a good end. "Human virtues are firm attitudes, stable dispositions, habitual perfections of intellect and will that govern our actions, order our passions, and guide our conduct according to reason and faith" (*CCC* 1804). The more talented or powerful a person is, the greater the impact he or she can have – for good or for evil. It all depends on how he or she uses it.

So let us pretend we are a coach looking for good players who are also good people. What do they look like? Are there only two kinds of players: those who practice virtue and those who practice vice? No, it is not that easy. Most of us are a combination of imperfect virtues and vices, just as we are combinations of different physical characteristics.

Whatever our physical combinations may be, there is still the missing ingredient of character to consider. It is not unusual for people to overcome their physical limitations through the acquisition of virtue. A recent movie told of a time when a person's place in society was determined by their genetic characteristics.[2] This determinism resulted in an unfair prejudice against people with weak genetic constitutions.

Here, a young man who had less than perfect genes was denied his lifelong ambition of joining the space program. Undaunted, he went to great extremes to overcome his natural limitations and the injustice of his situation. To make a long story short, he fooled the genetic testers to gain admission to the program and ended up being very successful. The point of the story was summed up in its subtitle: "There is no gene for the human spirit." We have a body, but we also have a spiritual soul that transcends the physical realm. We are born with our talents, but we make our character.

The Cardinal Virtues
There are names for the different ways we can show other-centered love. "Each (virtue) corresponds to a certain diverse state of the affection of love itself."[3] Although there are many virtues, there are four that are of vital importance because without them we are unable to practice any of the others. Historically these have been called the cardinal virtues; "cardinal" is a Latin word meaning hinge. Just as a door depends on a hinge to open, the quality of our hearts depend on the cardinal virtues. "Four virtues play a pivotal role and accordingly are called 'cardinal'; all the others are grouped around them. They are prudence, justice, fortitude, and temperance" (*CCC* 1805).

Okay, back to our question, "What kind of character would a coach look for?" First of all, a coach would look for players who know what to do and when to do it. Doing the right thing is good, but we also have to do it at the right time. For example, a quarterback throwing a pass on third and long is good, but throwing it long when the other team is blitzing is generally a bad idea. There is usually not enough time to complete a pass of that length. Clearly, such a play would not be wise on his part.

Prudence

Prudence is necessary for practicing all the other virtues. Do you remember those old movies with the chariot races? Prudence has been compared to the charioteer who holds the reins directing each horse of the team towards the finish line. For example, the horses on the outside generally needed more encouragement to run swiftly, while the horses on the inside needed to be more reserved.
However, there were times when the opposite was true; it was the charioteer's job to know when and how to reverse the order. In our case, prudence directs the other virtues towards achieving what is best for us.

We need to be prudent if we want to be happy. Prudence puts our thoughts and actions together in a way that is best under the circumstances. "The prudent man determines and directs his conduct in accordance with his judgment. With the help of this virtue we apply moral principles to particular cases without error and overcome doubts about the good to achieve and the evil to avoid" (*CCC* 1806). The opposite of this is imprudence, which is acting without thinking. Such behavior is rash and reckless.

Prudence, or wisdom as it is sometimes called, "is the virtue that disposes practical reason to discern our true good in every circumstance and choose the right means of achieving it; 'the prudent man looks where he is going'" (*CCC* 1806). In our example, the quarterback failed to properly evaluate the situation. If he had, he would have thrown the ball differently.

Prudence should not to be confused with being timid or cowardly. This is the opposite of acting without thinking. It is thinking, without acting. There are times when throwing long is the best thing to do, and throwing short is taking the easy way out. Prudence is the virtue that helps our quarterback make the right throw.

Justice

Okay, let's say we found a prudent quarterback. Is that all we need, or are there other virtues we should look for? What if our guy made a habit of taking all the credit but none of the blame? This would not be good, would it? This would show that he lacked the virtue of justice, which is another one of the cardinal virtues. "Justice is the moral virtue that consists in the constant and firm will to give their due to God and neighbor. Justice toward God is called the 'virtue of religion.' Justice toward men disposes one to respect the rights of each and to establish in human relationships the harmony that promotes equity with regard to persons and to the common good" (*CCC* 1807).

Taking all the credit for good plays, while denying any of the blame for bad ones, is not only unjust, it is foolish. Will the offensive lineman want to protect him anymore? Will the wide receivers be as willing to risk their health by trying to catch his poorly thrown passes? It is not likely. A just person makes sure everybody gets what he or she deserves. In this case, the linemen deserved some credit for blocking and allowing the quarterback time to pass, and the receiver deserved credit for actually catching it.

A coach with an unjust quarterback risks losing team harmony. Players may stop cooperating with one another. This can be deadly, because without teamwork you cannot win. Justice is the virtue that allows different parts to work together as an integrated whole. With justice, people are able to live together in peace.

Fortitude

The virtue of fortitude might not seem like a big deal, but when called by its other name – courage – its desirability is a no-brainer. Courage is the virtue that allows us to do what is right even when it is difficult. "Fortitude is the moral virtue that ensures firmness in difficulties and constancy in the pursuit of the good. It strengthens the resolve to resist temptations and to overcome obstacles in the moral life. The virtue of fortitude enables one to conquer fear, even fear of death, and to face trials and persecutions. It disposes one even to renounce and sacrifice his life in defense of a just cause" (*CCC* 1808).

Courage is the virtue that gives athletes the power to make the sacrifices necessary to reach their goals. It is the virtue that controls fear and enables us to face danger with firmness and presence of mind. All coaches are looking for this virtue. Courage would give our quarterback the power to hang in there and pass the ball even when he is under heavy pressure.

Courage is a valuable virtue in our personal lives as well. In order to do what is right, we must have the power to be different. Don't you think its funny how everybody claims to be different, when in fact they just follow the crowd? Sure, they may wear a different colored shirt, or have a different favorite band, but they all think and act the same. Their first concern is, "What is everybody else doing?" instead of asking, "What is the right thing to do?"

Courage is the power to do what is right no matter what anyone else thinks. It is a sign of life. "A dead thing can go with the stream, but only a living thing can go against it."[4] Courage also helps us to overcome difficulties in acquiring and practicing the other virtues. That is why it is called a "cardinal" virtue.

Temperance
Okay, so now we have a quarterback who is talented and also prudent because he does the right thing at the right time. He is also just because he gives credit where credit is due, and he is courageous enough to play under pressure. Is there anything more we should look for? Let's see how the fourth and last cardinal virtue could apply. Its name is temperance, and it is sometimes known as moderation.

"Temperance is the moral virtue that moderates the attraction of pleasures and provides balance in the use of created goods. It ensures the will's mastery over instincts and keeps desires within the limits of what is honorable" (*CCC* 1809). For example, to stretch our quarterback analogy a bit, temperance allows our man to throw the right distance; not too long and not too short, but right on target. He may stand in there courageously, in order to prudently throw the right pass, but he also has to throw it at an appropriate velocity. He might even have a cannon for an arm, but he shouldn't always throw the football as hard as he can. If he did, he would not complete many passes, and his arm would wear out too quickly. There we have it, the four cardinal virtues as they are modeled in our imaginary quarterback. Because of his virtue, his talents worked together harmoniously. This not only made him a good player, but it helped to make a good team.

These illustrations are useful only as far as they underscore the role virtue plays in our everyday lives. Whether we play sports or not, virtues are important to all of us. If we want to be a good person and have good friends, then we need to love others in an appropriate way. Virtue gives us this power. The four cardinal virtues we discussed are the hinges upon which all the other virtues hang. There are many other virtues. Let's discuss a few of them right now.

Care

Care is a virtue that springs from our realizing that we are in this together, and that we share a certain solidarity with others. "The inability to care, more than anything else, shows a human being to be inhuman. This is because caring for others is so fundamental to human nature as to coincide with it. To care is to express humanness. Not to care is to place a barrier between oneself and one's humanity."[5] The virtue of care gives us the power to overcome the inconvenience and sometime hassle involved with helping others.

Chastity

Chastity gives us the power to use our sexuality in a way that is in our best interest. It helps us to see the big picture. St. Thomas Aquinas saw that the lack of chastity caused blindness of mind, rashness, thoughtlessness, inconstancy, inordinate self-love, hatred of God, excessive love of this world, and abhorrence or despair of a future world.[6] Most troubling is that an unchaste person loses the sense of right and wrong. They will even use others in order to save themselves. Not exactly a trait we like to see in our friends, is it?

"Chastity is a most honorable virtue. It honors the self as well as the other. It may be a difficult virtue to attain, not because sexual desire is so intense, but because it is constantly being aroused....Aquinas, long before there were mass media understood only too well the dangerous role environmental seduction could play: 'There is not much sinning because of natural desires...But the stimuli of desire which man's cunning has devised are something else, and for the sake of these sins one sins very much,'[7] Doesn't this sound like the world we are living in now? Sex is one of the favorite "hooks" of the advertising world. Can you think of any examples? Did sex have anything to do with these products?

Compassion

Compassion is sharing the suffering of others. It is being there for them, and listening to them with empathy. When friends are compassionate, it feels as though they are helping us carry our burden. The joy of experiencing their love lessens our suffering.

67

Courtesy

Courtesy is having good manners, and treating people as if they were valuable, respected and important. It is infectious. Our expression of love can actually make people nicer and more agreeable. This is a virtue we can exercise daily with people we don't even know. Saying "please," "thank-you," and letting others into traffic are little ways we show love to those around us. This little virtue makes life more pleasant, and helps us to live in harmony.

Fidelity

Fidelity is the virtue that allows us to keep our commitments, even when it is difficult, and the outcome uncertain. It perseveres courageously, in faith, and in the hope that things will work out for the best. This is very important in relationships, especially in marriage. That is why it is important to make commitments carefully, and not rashly.

Responsibility

"To respond is to answer. Correspondingly, to be responsible is to be answerable, to be accountable. Irresponsible behavior is immature behavior. Taking responsibility – being responsible – is a sign of maturity."[8]

As we discussed earlier, we are born with natural tendencies, but we can never use this as an excuse for bad behavior. "That's just the way I am!" is not an excuse for inconsiderate or bad behavior. Nor is it even an accurate description, for we are never just what we are. "As Aristotle was among the first to insist, we become what we are as persons by the decisions that we ourselves make."[9] In other words, we are born with our talents, but we make our character.

Generosity

Generosity is giving things of value to other people. It is the opposite of greed. Being generous increases our capacity to love. Through the proper use of things, we are able to strengthen our hearts and build relationships with God and others. Jesus said, "If you wish to be perfect, go, sell what you have and give to [the] poor, and you will have treasure in heaven. Then come, follow me." (Mt 19:21). Please note that it is not our "stuff" that Jesus wants; he wants our hearts. Being generous helps put our hearts in the right place.

Graciousness

Graciousness is the virtue of remembering those who are not as "important" as us. Have you ever been ignored by somebody who thought they were better than you? A person who ignored you in order to hang out with the "cool" crowd? It feels lousy, doesn't it? Not only do you feel bad, but the offender looks bad. Being "stuck-up" is pretty obnoxious. A gracious person follows the Scriptures' command to treat rich and poor with the respect due them as human beings, and not according to what they can do for us. This applies to social differences as well as economic ones.

"My brothers, show no partiality as you adhere to the faith in our glorious Lord Jesus Christ. For if a man with gold rings on his fingers and in fine clothes comes into your assembly, or a poor person in shabby clothes also comes in, and you pay attention to the one wearing fine clothes and say, 'sit here, please' while you say to the poor one, 'sit there' or 'sit at my feet,' have you not made distinctions among yourselves and become judges with evil designs?" (Jas 2:1-4).

Humility

Humility is the virtue of seeing ourselves as we really are in relation to God and to others. It is living our lives according to this realistic assessment and not thinking more or less of ourselves then we ought. This is difficult because we are prone to swing to either extreme. We tend towards pride when we do well, and we get too down on ourselves when we don't. Humility is an important virtue. Since we are children of God we should make every effort to know ourselves so we can be effective in serving him. Scripture says, "The reward of humility and fear of the Lord is riches, honor and life" (Prv 22:4).

Integrity

Integrity is the virtue of being the person we claim to be. It is "walking the talk," or "practicing what we preach." We cannot carry a Bible or go to Mass on Sunday, and then sin with abandon the rest of the week, and still be a person of integrity. If we think we can, we are only fooling ourselves. To be honest means to be real, genuine and authentic. This shows respect for ourselves and for others.

Grade
9

Some believe deceiving others is all right so long as you are not caught. This may work some of the time, but not always. Scripture says, "He who walks honestly walks securely, but he whose ways are crooked will fare badly" (Prv 10:9). Caught or not, we should care more about who we are as persons. St. Thomas More is quoted as saying that we hold ourselves in our hands like sand; if we let go for a moment we are lost, never to regain ourselves.

One often hears politicians say they are opposed to abortion, but fail to exercise their authority to stop it. This shows a lack of integrity. Being two-faced might be clever, but avoiding moral obligations is a vice, not a virtue. How can you relate with someone who is not what they appear to be? Honesty is absolutely necessary for friendship.

Modesty
"The modest person does not draw undue attention to himself. He is self-assured, but not self-absorbed. He is temperate in dress, language and comportment, and has a strong sense of the value of his privacy. He knows that being a person is fundamentally incompatible with being an object for public consumption."[10] It is the opposite of some athletes who seem to work harder getting attention after a play than during it. They prance around waving wildly.

You may think such behavior is absurd and far removed from our daily lives, but it really isn't. Even though we don't thrash about like a football player, we sometimes dress for the same reason. "Wow, I want a piece of that!" is not a typical response to a modestly dressed person. Quite the contrary, "covering our body means that it is kept under our control, that it is available to no one but ourselves."[11] People who dress immodestly look as if they were objects for public consumption. Hence they shouldn't be surprised if they are used up and thrown away like any other consumable product. To avoid this, we should dress so people desire to *know* us better, not use us. Remember, objects are used; only persons are known and loved.

Patience
Patience is the virtue of quietly overcoming the difficulties we encounter. It helps us to keep our composure during stressful situations. It is much like the virtue of courage in that it requires strength, but patience is more subdued. It is one of the "fruits of

the Spirit which are perfections that the Holy Spirit forms in us as the first fruits of eternal glory. The tradition of the Church lists twelve of them: 'charity, joy, peace, patience, kindness, goodness, generosity, gentleness, faithfulness, modesty, self-control, chastity" (*CCC* 1832).

Patriotism

Patriotism pertains to our relationship with others as fellow countrymen. Like piety, which describes our relationship with our families and Church, patriotism describes our relationship with our country. It acknowledges our country as a gift, but also as a responsibility. Countries are natural arrangements of people that protect families and the rights of persons.

We should not take our country lightly. Many have even given their lives safeguarding the rights and freedoms we enjoy today. Countries are a means of upholding important truths about their people. For example, in the United States, our country is founded upon a Constitution that embodies our values as a nation.

True patriotism has often been misunderstood and distorted by unscrupulous leaders. Governments should not manipulate their people to behave unjustly and disguise it as duty. For example, St. Thomas More was beheaded for not obeying King Henry VIII. Although St. Thomas had served the king faithfully for many years in the highest offices, he refused to break God's law in order to obey the king. St. Thomas' last words were, "I die the king's good servant, but the Lord's first."

Other virtues

There are as many natural virtues as there are ways to communicate love. These are but a few. Can you think of any others?

The Theological Virtues

Jesus said, "Apart from me you can do nothing" (Jn 15:5). We are mistaken if we think we will become perfectly virtuous persons through our own efforts. Virtue alone will not get us into heaven. We need supernatural help to perfect our natural virtues, and to gain salvation. "Unless we 'seek first the kingdom of God and his righteousness,' all these other things will not be added to us…without the supernatural virtues, the natural virtues fail."[12]

Grade
9

The supernatural virtues are also known as the theological virtues "which are the foundation of Christian moral activity; they animate it and give it its special character. They inform and give life to the moral virtues. They are infused by God into the souls of the faithful to make them capable of acting as his children and of meriting eternal life....There are three theological virtues: faith, hope, and charity" (*CCC* 1813). These virtues are infused in us at baptism and they give us faith in God's word, hope in his promises, and love of God and neighbor.

Faith
"Faith is the theological virtue by which we believe in God and believe all that he has said and revealed to us, and that Holy Church proposes for our belief, because he is truth itself. By faith 'man freely commits his entire self to God.' For this reason the believer seeks to know and do God's will. 'The righteous shall live by faith.' Living faith 'works through charity'" (*CCC* 1814).

It is our faith that moves us to acquire the natural virtues, and to strive to be perfect as God is perfect. One of the misunderstandings among some Christians is this relationship between faith and works. "The answer to the faith and works issue is essentially a simple one, in fact, startlingly simple. It is that faith works. The whole complex question of reconciling Paul's words on faith and James' words on works, and of solving the dispute that sparked the Reformation, the dispute about justification by faith, is answered at its core at a single stroke: the very same 'living water' of God's own Spirit, God's own life in our soul, is received by faith and lived out by virtuous works."[13]

Hope
"Hope is the theological virtue by which we desire the kingdom of heaven and eternal life as our happiness, placing our trust in Christ's promises and relying not on our own strength, but on the help of the grace of the Holy Spirit," (*CCC* 1817). "The virtue of hope responds to the aspiration to happiness which God has placed in the heart of every man; it takes up the hopes that inspire men's activities and purifies them so as to order them to the kingdom of heaven" (*CCC* 1818).

Charity

The virtue of charity is also known as the virtue of love. It "is the theological virtue by which we love God above all things for his own sake, and our neighbor as ourselves for the love of God" (*CCC* 1822). "If I ...have not charity, says the Apostle, I am nothing. Charity is superior to all the virtues" (*CCC* 1826). Love perfects all of the other virtues, both human and theological. Even if we acquire all the virtues, they will not be perfect without love.

In summary, our particular circumstances bring about our growth in virtues. Every day we have opportunities to love God and others. Through our loving actions we grow in a particular virtue, but also in other virtues as well, because the virtues are all related. At first it will be difficult, but after a while it will become something we do without even thinking about it. Then we can happily claim to have acquired another virtue.

"Thou shall love the lord your God with thy whole heart, with thy whole soul and with thy whole mind."
This is the commandment of our great God, and he cannot command the impossible. Love is a fruit in season at all times and within the reach of every hand. Anyone may gather it and no limit is set. Everyone can reach this love through meditation, spirit of prayer, and sacrifice, by an intense inner life.

- Mother Teresa

Grade
9

Questions
1. What is virtue?
   Virtue is an habitual and firm disposition to do the good.

2. What is a cardinal virtue?
   A cardinal virtue is one of four virtues upon which all other virtues depend. They are prudence, justice, fortitude and charity.

3. What is the difference between human virtues and theological virtues?
   God infuses theological virtues at baptism, while human virtues are acquired by our own efforts.

4. Which virtue is the greatest, and why?
   Love is the greatest of all virtues because it lasts forever.

Notes
[1] Recounted by Coach Bill Parcells at New York Giants team meeting, 1985.
[2] *Gattaca*, 1997.
[3] St. Thomas Aquinas quoting St. Augustine, *Summa Theologiae* I-II, 61, 4.
[4] G.K. Chesterton, *The Everlasting Man*.
[5] Donald DeMarco, *The Heart of Virtue*, p. 21.
[6] Thomas Aquinas, *Summa Theologiae*, II-II,153, 5.
[7] DeMarco, *The Heart of Virtue*, pp. 32-33.
[8] William J. Bennett, *The Book of Virtues*, p. 185.
[9] *Ibid.* p. 186.
[10] DeMarco, *The Heart of Virtue*, p 168.
[11] David Isaacs, *Character Building*, p.109.
[12] Peter Kreeft, *Back to Virtue*, 72.
[13] *Ibid.* p. 67.

CHAPTER 6/7

People Are Created Within Relationships

Our Relationship with Our Family

Our families are a great gift. We might not always think of them in this way, but it is true. They provide us a unique opportunity to give and receive love.

As important as they are, they are beyond our control. Just as we did not choose to be born, we did not choose our families. It is similar to being drafted in professional baseball. A player must report to the team that drafts him. Even if he is a life-long Yankees fan, if the Red Sox draft him, he must go to Boston. This then becomes an opportunity for him to grow in any number of virtues, which he would have otherwise missed. Hardships make us stronger if we let them. Who knows? He may even learn to like being a Red Sox.

The same can be said for our family. We can wish they were different or we can learn to enjoy them just as they are. Even though our families can be a source of irritation at times, they can help us to grow in character. We should pause and wonder over these mysterious bonds. They are really a great blessing. We may soon realize that God places us in families because he loves us. And even if they are imperfect, good can still come of it.

Admittedly, we are living at a time when family life has become weakened by a great number of things, many of which are being discussed in this curriculum. Many families are suffering from very serious problems. These are problems that our Lord does not want to happen, but since he gave us a free will he allows them to happen.

Even though many of us have made bad choices, he is also there to help us overcome them. If we are born into a difficult family situation, we can turn to him, and hope for the day when we will be able to make a family of our own.

Our beginning

It is God's plan that we are born into families where the bond is giving-love, and not contractual. This is contrary to some teachers who explain our existence as being one of autonomous individuals making social contracts with one another.[1] The true nature of our beginning is being born of love, and into love – not entering into a personal services contract with our mothers.

What is a family?

Unfortunately we have gotten in the habit of calling most any happy group or community "family." While this may add substance to the group, it does so at the expense of true families. It can make families seem commonplace when in fact they are really quite extraordinary.

A family is a community which is established upon the consent of the spouses. It is a man and a woman united in marriage, together with their children. This should be considered the normal reference point by which the different forms of family relationships are evaluated.

"Marriage and the family are ordered to the good of the spouses and to the procreation and education of children. The love of the spouses and the begetting of children create among members of the same family personal relationships and primordial responsibilities. Its members are persons equal in dignity. Moreover, for the good of its members and of society, the family necessarily has many responsibilities, rights, and duties" (*CCC* 2201-2203).

Piety

Piety is a virtue that helps us to understand and benefit from the relationship with our family. Piety is respect for God's design in creation, and the family is most certainly God's design for the human race.

"Piety is a profound respect for the forces that preceded us and brought us into being. It is reverence for God, nature, and parents. By means of piety, a person remains united with what is good in his past, what is valuable and helpful in his tradition."[2]

Piety is an antidote for the alienation so many of us experience today. Through it we realize that we are connected, and that we do not stand alone. It gives us hope that our setbacks may serve to help those who come after us.

Piety helps us to answer the questions we asked in Chapter 1, "Who am I?" and "Where am I going?" It knows that who we are is who we were. Piety raises the important question, "Where have I come from?" Understanding God's plan for family life helps us to answer these important questions.

The Fourth Commandment

The only aspect of family life that hints of a contractual arrangement is the Covenant God offered us in the Ten Commandments. The Fourth Commandment states, "Honor your father and your mother, that you may have a long life in the land which the Lord, your God, is giving you" (Ex 20:12, Dt 5:16). "God has willed that, after him, we should honor our parents to whom we owe life and who have handed on to us the knowledge of God. We are obliged to honor and respect all those whom God, for our good, has vested with his authority" (*CCC* 2197).

Although this commandment addresses the parent-child relationship, it concerns ties with extended family and much more. "It requires honor, affection, and gratitude toward elders and ancestors. Finally, it extends to the duties of pupils to teachers, employees to employers, subordinates to leaders, citizens to their country, and to those who administer or govern it" (*CCC* 2199).

Like the farm system of professional baseball, the family is the place where we prepare for the "big leagues." It is a place where we learn to grow in virtue. Through the example and instruction of those who love us, we are able to grow in the power of self-giving.

Grade
10

The duties of children towards their parents
The respect children owe their parents "derives from gratitude towards those who, by the gift of life, their love and their work, have brought their children into the world and enabled them to grow in stature, wisdom, and grace" (*CCC* 2215). "As long as a child lives at home with his parents, the child should obey his parents in all that they ask him when it is for his good or that of his family. Children should also obey the reasonable directions of their teachers and all to whom their parents have entrusted them. But if a child is convinced in conscience that it would be morally wrong to obey a particular order, he must not do so."

"As they grow up, children should continue to respect their parents. They should anticipate their wishes, willingly seek their advice, and accept their just admonitions. Obedience towards parents ceases with the emancipation of the children; not so respect, which is always owed to them" (*CCC* 2217). This duty of gratitude includes helping parents with "material and moral support in old age and in times of illness, loneliness, or distress" (*CCC* 2218). This respect "promotes harmony in all of family life; it also concerns relationships between brothers and sisters" (*CCC* 2219).

What are some of the ways you can show the members of your family respect?

The duties of parents towards their children
For their part, "Parents must regard their children as children of God and respect them as human persons. Showing themselves obedient to the will of the Father in heaven, they educate their children to fulfill God's law" (*CCC* 2222).

Just as a coaching staff's responsibility is to prepare the team to play, parents prepare their children not only for this life, but also for the one to come. "Parents have the first responsibility for the education of their children. They bear witness to this responsibility first by creating a home where tenderness, forgiveness, respect, fidelity, and disinterested service are the rule. The home is well suited for education in the virtues. This requires an apprenticeship in self-denial, sound judgment, and self-mastery – the preconditions of all true freedom.

"Parents should teach their children to subordinate the 'material and instinctual dimensions to interior and spiritual ones.' Parents have a grave responsibility to give good example to their children. By knowing how to acknowledge their own failings to their children, parents will be better able to guide and correct them" (*CCC* 2223). Even though they have different roles to play, parents and children share the role of pilgrims on their way to their heavenly home. They should help each other with the care and respect due each of them. After all, we are in this together.

The power and privilege of parenthood

The foremost duty and privilege of parents is the education of their children. Parents have a powerful influence on a child's relationship with God. John Cardinal O'Connor shared one of his childhood experiences as an example: "Does every kid have an older sister who keeps telling him he's adopted? I sure did. She's the same one who told me on a late Christmas Eve that Santa Claus was downstairs in our kitchen with his whiskers caught in the gas range. That worried me a great deal. That I had allegedly been left in a basket on the front doorstep and taken into the family didn't worry me in the slightest. On the contrary, it made me feel special. In fact, I couldn't wait to tell my mother and father!

"I remember the day I did. My father looked me right in the eye and put his hand on my little shoulder. His answer was as important to the rest of my life as anything I have ever heard since. 'This is your mother, son, and I'm your father. You were born in the house. But if we had found you in a basket on the doorstep, we would have been proud to bring you in and love you as much as we do now.' That's called security. I have always been grateful to my sister that she raised the question.

"There's a difference now. I no longer have to think little-boy thoughts about what to get my father for Father's Day. I always offer Mass for him, of course, which he liked most when I was a young priest before he died. But apart from that, I spend much of the day grateful for what he gave me; the trust I felt in him was the begin-ning of my trust in God. Of that, I am certain. I could always believe my father. He never told less than the truth."[3]

Mr. O'Connor probably had no idea that his words would impact so many souls. In his simple act of love and obedience, he formed not only his son but also everyone his son has ever touched, which is a considerable number given the size of his responsibilities as Cardinal Archbishop of New York. A similar truth is expressed in the adage "The hand that rocks the cradle rules the world." This eloquently explains a mother's influence in the world. Even though she may never enter public life herself, her children may. More than anything else parents impact the world through their children.

Indeed, the *Catechism* calls the family the "Original cell of social life. It is the natural society in which husband and wife are called to give themselves in love and in the gift of life. Authority, stability, and a life of relationships within the family constitute the foundations for freedom, security, and fraternity within society. The family is the community in which, from childhood, one can learn moral values, begin to honor God, and make use of freedom. Family life is an initiation into the life of society" (*CCC* 2207).

The family in society
The family is also God's instrument of love towards society. "The family should live in such a way that its members learn to care and take responsibility for the young, the old, the sick, the handicapped, and the poor" (*CCC* 2208). God demonstrates his love for us through a family that provides for our spiritual, emotional and physical needs. We are social beings; not autonomous individuals that are capable of being sociable. We need what only families can give us - love.

Although governments can help by providing things families usually provide, they do so imperfectly. Governments need families, because the state does not have the resources to nurture and care for all of its citizens properly. Only the family can form responsible citizens who will be able to strengthen the community. There is no substitute for love.

As the family goes, so goes society. Knowing this, wise governments have supported the institution of the family. They know that strong families make for a strong community. "The family must be helped and defended by appropriate social measures. Where families cannot fulfill their responsibilities, other social bodies have the duty of helping them and of supporting the institution of the family. Following the principle of subsidiarity, larger communities should take care not to usurp the family's prerogatives or interfere in its life" (*CCC* 2209).

The principle of subsidiarity means "a community of a higher order should not interfere in the internal life of a community of a lower order, depriving the latter of its functions, but rather should support it in case of a need and help to co-ordinate its activity with activities of the rest of society, always with a view to the common good" (*CCC* 1883).

This principle of subsidiarity is an important one because it protects our freedom. It prevents busybodies from taking over our lives and doing things that we are able to do for ourselves. Most often our way is the best way, because we are closer to the situation then anyone else. Government officials are often too far removed to make informed decisions. For them, it would be like calling the plays when they aren't even watching the game. "The family is the test of freedom; because the family is the only thing that the free man makes for himself and by himself."[4]

Questions

1. What is the Fourth Commandment?

   Honor your father and your mother that your days may be long in the land which the Lord your God gives you.

2. What is the virtue of piety?

   Piety is respect for God's design in creation, and for the forces that precede us and brought us into being. It is reverence for God, nature and parents.

3. What is the basic unit of society?

   The family is the basic unit of society.

4. What is a family?

   A man and a woman united in marriage, together with their children form a family.

5. What is the principle of subsidiarity?

   Subsidiarity is a practical principle that dictates that public tasks be performed by the lowest possible level of government. For example, the state is to carry out the work of education only when parents and smaller groups are unable to do so.

Notes

[1] See generally the Enlightenment philosophers Hobbes, Locke, Rousseau, et. al.

[2] Donald DeMarco, *The Heart of Virtue*, p. 184.

[3] John Cardinal O'Connor, *On Being Catholic*, pp. 19-20.

[4] G.K. Chesterton, "The Home of the Unities," in *The New Witness*, January 17, 1919.

CHAPTER 6/7

People Are Created Within Relationships

Our Relationship with the Church

We have a relationship with Jesus as members of his Church. Jesus spoke of the close relationship between him and those who would follow him: "Abide in me, and I in you... . I am the vine, you are the branches" (Jn 15:4-5). And he proclaimed a real communion between his own body and ours, "He who eats my flesh and drinks my blood abides in me, and I in him" (Jn 6:56). In this chapter we will explore the nature of this communion.

Throughout this curriculum we have used sports as a way to explain the truth about things. However, sporting metaphors do a poor job of communicating the awesome mystery of the Church. To say that the kingdom of God is like winning the World Cup is silly. Clearly, membership in his Church is more excellent than being a member of the world's best soccer team. A championship lasts for a year, sainthood is eternal.

A peek at the eternal

Things that are true, beautiful and good are all reflections of God. We know this from the world around us. God is known through his creation. "For since the creation of the world his invisible attributes, his invisible power and divine nature, have been clearly seen, being understood through what has been made...." (Rom 1: 20). In short, we see something of the eternal in the things around us.

Our culture is a reflection of our perception of reality. Our art tries to capture the truth of what our senses perceive; it tries "to interpret its hidden mystery."[1] The idea of greatness hidden within the ordinary is best illustrated by the Incarnation of Christ. Jesus, the Son of God, was "hidden" as a human child within a humble Jewish family. "If the Son of God had come into the world of visible realities …then by analogy, a representation of the mystery could be used...."[2]

Hence, "every genuine art form in its own way is a path to the inmost reality of man and of the world."[3] That is why the Church has certain looks, sounds and smells. Things like architecture, vestments, bells, incense, liturgy, all have a meaning and a purpose. They point to realities that our five senses cannot detect on their own, but exist nevertheless.

In fact, they can be more real than what our senses can detect. A writer once remarked that the reason angels were able to pass through walls wasn't because they were vaporous and insubstantial, but rather because they were more real than the walls themselves.[4] If done prayerfully and tastefully, the external signs of the Church can turn our gaze towards the higher and more real things they represent.

Imperfect but holy

An artist's success can be measured by his or her ability to wed the beautiful and the true, "so that through art…souls might be lifted up from the world of the senses to the eternal."[5] However, just as an artist's work often falls short of the perfection of his or her original inspiration, so too the Church is less than the perfection willed by God. The reason for this is not because God is a limited craftsman like the human artist, but rather he is hampered by our lack of cooperation with him.

The Church is comprised of sinners. Jesus said he came to heal sinners like a doctor heals the sick (Matt 9:6). If we come to church expecting to find it filled with perfect people we will be disappointed. Instead of expecting Heaven where everyone is perfect, we should expect to walk into a hospital filled with people suffering from various illnesses.

"Christ, holy, innocent, and undefiled, knew nothing of sin, but came only to expiate the sins of the people. The Church, however, clasping sinners to her bosom, at once holy and always in need of purification, follows constantly the path of penance and renewal. All members of the Church, including her ministers, must acknowledge that they are sinners. In everyone, the weeds of sin will still be mixed with the good wheat of the Gospel until the end of time. Hence the Church gathers sinners already caught up in Christ's salvation but still on the way to holiness" (CCC 827).

One with Christ

The Church is one with Christ, and the saints are acutely aware of this unity. St. Augustine said, "Let us rejoice then and give thanks that we have become not only Christians, but Christ himself. Do you understand and grasp brethren, God's grace toward us? Marvel and rejoice: we have become Christ. For if he is the head, we are the members; he and we together are the whole man" (CCC 795).

Moreover, Pope St. Gregory the Great said, "Our redeemer has shown himself to be one person with the holy church whom he has taken to himself." Similarly St. Thomas Aquinas added, "Head and members form as it were one and the same mystical person." Finally, the *Catechism* recounts a reply given by St. Joan of Arc to her judges which sums it up nicely: "About Jesus Christ and the Church, I simply know they're just one thing, and we shouldn't complicate the matter" (CCC 795).

The Church as Bride

Jesus referred to himself as the "bridegroom," and the Church and its individual members as a bride betrothed to him.[6] St. Paul speaks beautifully of this betrothal when he says, "Christ loved the Church and gave himself up for her, that he might sanctify her."[7] It is interesting to note that St. Paul uses the marriage relationship between a man and a woman to describe the relationship between Christ and his Church.

This is not an exaggeration. Do you know that marriage is also modeled upon the relationship of the Holy Trinity?[8] It is true. The love between the husband and wife results in another person – their child. Similarly, the love between Father and Son is another person – the Holy Spirit.

Understanding the deep significance of marriage helps us to understand why divorce is to be avoided. "Divorce does injury to the covenant of salvation, of which sacramental marriage is the sign" (*CCC* 2384). "Divorce is immoral also because it introduces disorder into the family and into society. This disorder brings grave harm to the deserted spouse, to children traumatized by the separation of their parents and often torn between them, and because of its contagious effect which makes it truly a plague on society" (*CCC* 2385).

However, "It can happen that one of the spouses is the innocent victim of a divorce decreed by civil law; this spouse therefore has not contravened the moral law. There is a considerable difference between a spouse who has sincerely tried to be faithful to the sacrament of marriage and is unjustly abandoned, and one who through his own grave fault destroys a canonically valid marriage" (*CCC* 2386).

That is why it is so important for both men and women to build their marriages upon a relationship with Jesus. He wants marriages to be happy and is always present to help married couples overcome their inevitable difficulties. God has a plan for marriages, but we can only benefit from it when both are willing to follow him.

God's plan for the Church
You may ask, "How did all of this happen to me? I just kind of go to Church on Sunday – you know?" Good question, the answer is that the Catholic Church is more than just a sign or a symbol of higher things. She is a sacrament, which means she contains and communicates the invisible grace she signifies (*CCC* 774). A sacramental Church makes invisible relationships visible. The Church is the visible plan of God's love for humanity, because God desires that the whole human race may become one People of God, form one Body of Christ, and be built up into one temple of the Holy Spirit (*CCC* 776).

The Church began with the gathering of God's people after the relationship between God and man was broken by the sin of Adam and Eve. "The gathering together of the Church is, as it were, God's reaction to the chaos provoked by sin" (*CCC* 761). In the fullness of time, Jesus carried out the Father's plan of our salvation. Jesus began the Church by preaching the Good News. Those who welcomed his word welcomed the Kingdom of God itself.

Jesus also taught those who gathered around him how to live and how to pray in a new way. He also gave the Church a structure that will remain until the Kingdom is fully achieved. He chose the twelve Apostles, with Peter as their head; together they share Jesus' mission and power. Jesus spent much of his time preparing and building his Church (*CCC* 763-765).

When Jesus' work on earth was accomplished, he ascended into heaven and sent the Holy Spirit to direct the work of the Church through his various gifts. The Holy Spirit bestows upon the Church varied hierarchic and charismatic gifts enabling her to fulfill her mission (*CCC* 768). The Holy Spirit's role in the Church is so profound that Pentecost Sunday is sometimes called the "birthday of the Church."

Baptism is the gate
You may still be saying, "Okay, but how does all of that apply to me? How did I actually become the body of Christ?" Well, from the very day of Pentecost the Church has celebrated and administered holy baptism. This baptism is the gate by which we enter into the Church (*CCC* 950). "St. Peter declares to the crowd astounded by his preaching: 'Repent, and be baptized every one of you in the name of Jesus Christ for the forgiveness of your sins; and you shall receive the gift of the Holy Spirit.' The apostles and their collaborators offered Baptism to anyone who believed in Jesus" (*CCC* 1226). If you are baptized, then you are a member of the Church.

Communion of the saints
Baptism, along with all the other sacraments, binds us to Jesus and to one another (*CCC* 950). This is great news to people who are dispirited and alienated. Through baptism we become members of something bigger and better than anything the world has ever known. The Apostles Creed refers to this union as the communion of saints. "The communion of saints is the Church" (*CCC* 946). "But the most important member is Christ, since he is the head.... . Therefore, the riches of Christ are communicated to all the members, through the sacraments" (*CCC* 947).The *Catechism* lists the following as spiritual goods that each member shares with the other:

Communion in the faith. The faith of the faithful is the faith of the Church, received from the apostles. Faith is a treasure of life, which is enriched by being shared.

Communion of the sacraments. The communion of saints must be understood as the communion of the sacraments. The name communion can be applied to all of them, for they unite us to God. But this name is better suited to the Eucharist than to any other, because it is primarily the Eucharist that brings this communion about.

Communion of charisms. Within the communion of the Church, the Holy Spirit distributes special graces among the faithful of every rank for the building up of the Church. Now, "to each is given the manifestation of the Spirit for the common good" (1 Corinthians 12:7).

"They had everything in common" (Acts 4:32). Everything the true Christian has is to be regarded as a good possessed in common with everyone else. All Christians should be ready and eager to come to the help of the needy and of their neighbors in want. A Christian is a steward of the Lord's goods.

Communion in charity. "None of us lives to himself, and none of us dies to himself" (Rom 14:7). "If one member suffers, all suffer together; if one member is honored, all rejoice together. Now you are the body of Christ and individually members of it" (1 Cor 12:26-27). Because of our solidarity with both the living and the dead, our actions affect the others in our communion – both for good and bad (*CCC* 950-953).

Three states of the Church
The above statement about solidarity with the dead is not a misprint. There are three states of the one Church: those of us who are still pilgrims here on earth; others who have died and are being purified; those who are now in heaven. These are sometimes referred to as the Church Militant, Church Suffering, and Church Triumphant, respectively.

Our relationship to those in the Church is not interrupted by death; in fact it can be reinforced. We can pray for them, and they can pray for us. Our prayers are especially appreciated by those who are in the process of purification, because they are no longer able to pray for themselves. Our prayers for those undergoing purification helps to loosen them from their sins, and also to make their prayers for us effective (*CCC* 955, 958).

The prayerful intercession of those already in heaven is especially desirable because they are more closely united with Christ. Many great saints have spoken of their continued concern for others after their deaths. On his deathbed, St. Dominic told his brothers, "Do not weep, for I shall be more useful to you after my death and I shall help you then more effectively than during my life." The Little Flower, St. Therese of Lisieux, said, "I want to spend my heaven in doing good on earth" (*CCC* 956).

Friendship with the saints

Our devotion to the saints should also be one of friendship whereby our bonds with them in the Holy Spirit are strengthened. "Exactly as Christian communion among our fellow pilgrims brings us closer to Christ, so our communion with the saints joins us to Christ....We worship Christ as God's Son; we love the martyrs as the Lord's disciples and imitators, and rightly so because of their matchless devotion towards their king and master. May we also be their companions and fellow disciples!" (*CCC* 957).

Do you have a devotion to a particular saint or saints? If you don't, ask God for inspiration. Take a moment and make a list of some of the saints you are familiar with. What virtues are they known for? Why do you think they might be helpful to us?

If you ever looked at a book of the saints, you will note that they are all very different from one another. They are not cookie-cutter copies of one another. This is because God made us all different, for different purposes. Do you remember the 4 Principles of Life? God has a plan for the talents he's given to each of us. It is up to us to say "yes" to that plan. The Blessed Virgin Mary is a great example. "By her complete adherence to the Father's will, to his Son's redemptive work, and to every prompting of the Holy Spirit, the Virgin Mary is the Church's model of faith and charity" (*CCC* 967).

Happiness is living our vocation
This wide diversity of people reflects God's glory. Together we make up the body of Christ. Since God has a different plan for each one of us, it follows that we should all have different talents and abilities. The way in which we serve God will depend greatly upon our abilities and environment. Of course there is difficulty in discerning what God's plan is. Nevertheless, the natures and talents he gives us are clues. If he wants us to do something, he gives us the ability to do it.

Sometimes ambition and envy make us want to do something other than what God wants of us. This is especially evident today, when there are so many options and opportunities. We need to remind ourselves that what we want is happiness, not power, prestige, or money. We will only be happy if we are doing what we were made to do.

Let's return to our sporting metaphor for a moment. Suppose you were the coach of a world-class soccer team. You think everything is going great until your star goalie begins to think she is under-appreciated because she doesn't get to score any goals. You tell her she's crazy, and that it is just as important to stop the other team from scoring as it is to score. She counters by telling you she is quitting unless you let her play forward instead. You try to talk her out of it, but in the end you let her have her way. You give in because you don't want to lose her and upset the team even more.

As predicted, the team was much less successful. Opponents were scoring more often than before, and the former goalie could not make up for this deficit with scores of her own. At first she was happy because she got her way. But after the novelty wore off, she was embarrassed because she wasn't scoring as much as the other forwards in the league – no matter how hard she tried. She also became frustrated that she wasn't able to use her greatest asset – her strong, sure hands. Only goalies can use their hands in soccer.

At this point she had four options She could: quit the team altogether; make excuses and blame others for her lack of production; cheat by trying to use her hands; or she could do the honorable thing and return to the goal. If she did decide to return, the team should welcome her back, and the wayward goalie should apologize and try to make amends (perhaps by bringing the Gatorade and orange slices next time!).

The point is that everyone is happier when they are doing the things for which they are made. This is our vocation. Don't make the mistake of Adam and Eve who weren't satisfied with merely living in Paradise (can you imagine). No, they had to be like God; they wanted to make their own rules. They were not happy with the nature God had given them. They had allowed Satan to feed their discontent.

Different roles within the Church

Many of us likewise refuse to accept our natures and situations. We try to escape and become someone we are not. Moreover, we allow others to convince us we are miserable and under-appreciated. This not only hurts us, but everyone else in the Church as well, because we all share in the same spiritual goods. However, please note that this doesn't mean that we shouldn't work to improve and refine our talents. We must avoid complacency as well as envy. It takes prudence and humility to know which is which.

In order to serve the unity and mission of the Church, our Lord has willed a difference of ministry between its members while still sharing the same ultimate mission. Like a soccer team, each player plays a different position while sharing the same goal of winning. Did you ever watch youngsters play soccer? It is a mess. They run all over the place; there is no teamwork. Nobody plays his or her position correctly. That is what the Church looks like during times of confusion.

However the Church isn't ordered according to what we think is best. Rather it is ordered to what Christ himself thinks is best. He instituted the Church. He gave her authority and mission, orientation and goal: In order to shepherd the People of God and to increase its numbers without cease, Christ the Lord set up in his Church a variety of offices which aim at the good of the whole body (*CCC* 874).

These roles are divided between the hierarchy, the laity, and the consecrated life. The hierarchy has been entrusted with the office of teaching, sanctifying, and governing in Jesus' name and by his power. The laity exercise the priestly, prophetic, and kingly office of

Christ in their respective spheres of influence in everyday life. Finally, the consecrated are those, from both groups, who have consecrated themselves to God by taking vows of chastity, poverty and obedience (*CCC* 873). By virtue of their life in Christ there exists among all of them a true equality with regard to dignity and their activity according to each one's condition and function (*CCC* 872).

Ecumenical relationships

Has the sheer number of Christian churches ever confused you? Have you ever wondered why people who love Jesus do not all attend the same church? You are not alone. This situation has turned many people off to Christianity. Our example of disunity has prevented many from approaching Jesus in his Church.

The existence of different Christian denominations keeps others from knowing God. "Division openly contradicts the will of Christ, provides a stumbling block to the world, and inflicts damage on the most holy cause of proclaiming the Good News to every creature."[9] Jesus himself, at the hour of his Passion, "prayed that they may all be one" (Jn 17:21). This unity, "stands at the very heart of Christ's mission. It is not some secondary attribute of the community of his disciples. Rather, it belongs to the very essence of this community."[10]

Although the differences between Catholics, Protestants and Orthodox are real and important, the things that unite us are greater than those that divide us. "All those justified by faith through Baptism are incorporated into Christ. They therefore have a right to be honored by the title of Christian, and are properly regarded as brothers and sisters in the Lord by the sons and daughters of the Catholic Church."[11]

What can we do as individuals to improve our relationships with Christians, who are not in full communion with the Catholic Church? The *Catechism* lists certain requirements for responding to the call of ecumenism:
- A permanent renewal of the Church in greater fidelity to her vocation…

- Conversion of heart as the faithful 'try to live holier lives according to the Gospel'…

- Prayer in common, because 'change of heart and holiness of life, along with public and private prayer for the unity of Christians, should be regarded as the soul of the whole ecumenical movement'...

- Fraternal knowledge of each other;

- Ecumenical formation of the faithful and especially of priests;

- Dialogue among theologians and meetings among Christians of the different churches and communities;

- Collaboration among Christians in various areas of service to mankind...

(*CCC* 821).

The latter point on collaboration describes the work of Life Athletes very well. We are a coalition of professional and Olympic athletes who come from many different Christian traditions. While we are sometimes saddened that we are not "on the same page" religiously, our work together has helped us to grow in respect, understanding and love for one another.

We are hopeful that someday we will grow into full communion with one other as our Lord desires. In the meantime, this concern for achieving unity involves the whole Church, faithful and clergy alike. But we must realize that this requires more than just human powers. That is why we place all our hope in the prayer of Christ for the Church, in the love of the Father for us, and in the power of the Holy Spirit (*CCC* 822).

Questions

1. How can the Church be holy when there are so many imperfect people in it?
   The Church is holy because she is one with Jesus Christ, and Jesus Christ is holy.

2. What is God's plan for his Church?
   God's plan for the Church is that through her, the whole human race may become one People of God, form one Body of Christ, and be built up into the temple of the Holy Spirit.

3. What binds us to Jesus and the other members of the Church?
   Baptism, along with all the other sacraments, binds us to Jesus and to one another. This is especially true of the Eucharist.

4. Why did Jesus Christ create different roles for his followers?
   While everyone has the same ultimate mission, Jesus willed a difference of ministry in order to serve the order and mission of the Church.

5. Why are the saints good friends to have?
   Having relationships with saints helps us to follow their examples of saying "yes" to God's plan for our lives.

6. Why are good relationships with other Christians important?
   Good relations with Christians who are not Catholic is important because Jesus wants all of us to be one, and to bring the entire human race into the Church. It is helpful to remember that although our differences are real and important, there is still very much we have in common with one another.

7. Why is Mary a good model for us?
   Mary is a good model for us because she always said "yes" to God.

Notes

1. John Paul II, *The Way of Beauty: Letter of His Holiness Pope John Paul II to Artists*, 6.
2. *Ibid.*, 7.
3. *Ibid.*, 6.
4. C.S. Lewis.
5. John Paul II, *The Way of Beauty: Letter of His Holiness Pope John Paul II to Artists*, 7.
6. Mark 2:19, *CCC* 796; cf. Matthew 22:1-14; Matthew 25:1-13; 1 Corinthians 6:15-17; 2 Corinthians 11:2.
7. Ephesians 5: 25-26, *CCC* 796.
8. *CCC* 2205, *Familiaris Consortio*, 11.
9. Second Vatican Ecumenical Council, Decree on Ecumenism *Unitatis Redintegratio*, 1. *Ut Unum Sint*, 6.
10. *Ut Unum Sint*, 9.
11. Second Vatican Ecumenical Council, Decree on Ecumenism *Unitatis Redintegratio*, 1. *Ut Unum Sint*, 13.

CHAPTER 6/7

People Are Created Within Relationships

Our Relationship with the World

God has a plan for each of us. A plan that is closely related to the reason he made us, which is to know him, to love him, and to serve him in this life and to be happy with him in the next. We have also learned that knowing and loving others is what life is all about. Therefore, our relationships become the key to our happiness, because it is through them that we give and receive love. We also learned that virtue expresses our love in an appropriate way. It helps us to navigate the complexities of life and its relationships.

Chapters 6 and 7 are a reminder that we are social creatures, not merely "sociable." This is important because it helps us to understand ourselves better. We are not autonomous individuals. It is natural for us to be in relationship with others. "The first and basic expression of the social dimension of the person, then, is the married couple and the family: 'But God did not create man a solitary being. From the beginning male and female he created them.'"[1]

We are now going to discuss our relationship with the world beyond our family and the Church. We all recognize in ourselves a need for a wider community wherein each of us contributes. For this reason we set up various forms of political communities, which exist for the good of all.

The world is our vineyard

Pope John Paul II offers one of Jesus' parables as an illustration of

Grade
12

our relationship with the world. "For the kingdom of heaven is like a householder who went out early in the morning to hire laborers for his vineyard. After agreeing with the laborers for a denarius a day, he sent them into his vineyard" (Mt 20:1-2).

This parable sets before our eyes the Lord's vast vineyard and the women and men who are called and sent forth by him to labor in it. The vineyard is the whole world, which is to be transformed according to the plan of God in view of the final coming of the Kingdom of God.[2]

"And going out about the third hour he saw others standing idle in the marketplace; and he said to them, 'You too go into the vineyard' (Mt 20:3-4). From that distant day the call of the Lord Jesus 'You too go into my vineyard' never fails to resound in the course of history: it is addressed to every person who comes into this world."[3]

We are all a part of the team
When it comes to working in his vineyard, our Lord did not make distinctions between religious and lay people, wherein one group works, while the other watches. No, we are all in it together. Everyone in the Church has an active part to play in her mission and salvation. This is especially true today as we begin the Third Millennium. This a great moment in history that calls the lay faithful with particular urgency.[3]

Our dignity as Christians is the source of our motivation for working in the world. This status makes demands on us. Demands that are similar to the royal noblesse oblige where those of high rank have a duty to behave nobly towards others. More precisely, this dignity demands that we work in the Lord's vineyard: "Upon all the lay faithful, then, rests the exalted duty of working to assure that each day the divine plan of salvation is further extended to every person, of every era, in every part of the earth."[4]

Church and state
This mission does not necessarily conflict with our role as citizens of our country. Rather, in democracies such as the United States we have the opportunity to give substance to our political freedom by doing what ought to be done. "Democracy is not a substitute for morality....Its value stands-or falls-with the values which it embod-

ies and promotes."[5] Our founders understood that freedom must be ordered towards higher things, if the country were to survive.

Even though our country's founders believed in the sovereignty of God, the United States is not a theocracy where political power and religious authority are combined. "The political community and the church are autonomous and independent of each other in their own fields. Nevertheless, both are devoted to the personal vocation of man, though under different titles."[6]

In other words, they both work towards the common good, but from different vantage points. The common good embraces all those conditions of social life by which individuals, families and organizations can achieve more thoroughly their own fulfillment. This has made the United States hospitable to many generations of different religious groups and non-believers who found a home here. The tolerance of our system of government is rooted in the Judeo-Christian principle that all human beings share the same rights, no matter what their religious, cultural, or physical differences.

The central issue
Our form of government was created very different from others. That is why it is referred to as an experiment. There was no guarantee that it was going to work. Nevertheless, it is interesting to note that both the Church and the state agreed that this experiment be built upon the unchanging truths of the human person.

Our Declaration of Independence states, "We hold these truths to be self-evident, that all men are created equal, that they are endowed by their Creator with certain unalienable Rights, that among these are Life, Liberty, and the Pursuit of Happiness." This assertion agrees with the basis of our work in the Lord's vineyard, which is to rediscover and make others rediscover the dignity of every human person.

"The dignity of the person is the most precious possession of an individual. As a result, the value of one person transcends all the material world. The words of Jesus, 'For what does it profit a man to gain the whole world and to forfeit his life?' contain an enlightening and stirring statement about the individual: value comes not from what a person 'has' – even if the person possessed the whole world! – as much as from what a person 'is': the goods of the world do not count as much as the goods of the person, the good which is the person individually."[7]

Grade
12

Ending contradictions

It is comforting to note that our country was founded upon principles that are oriented towards the human good. However, practice often differs from theory, and we need to end the contradictions between the two. This is the work that awaits us in the vineyard. That is if we choose to go.

One such contradiction was the enslavement of Africans, which was eventually ended after a long hard struggle. Today, many other contradictions exist, but none of them threatens human dignity in the way abortion and euthanasia do. These are direct attacks on life itself, which is the fundamental human good. Without the right to life we cannot enjoy any other right. If we are dead, rights no longer matter.

That is why our government must be oriented towards the good of the people, and not towards mere productivity and cost-effectiveness. Otherwise the lives of the unborn, infirm, terminally ill, and other politically weak people will be at risk. The Catholic Bishops of the United States have cautioned us, "As we tinker with the beginning, the end and even the intimate cell structure of life, we tinker with our own identity as a free nation dedicated to the dignity of the human person. When American political life becomes an experiment on people rather than for and by them, it will no longer be worth conducting."[8]

Where do we begin?

Even though our founders believed in protecting human dignity, later generations like our own must be persuaded to do the same. Where do we begin? How do we make civil laws conform to the reality of human dignity? "For citizens and elected officials alike, the basic principle is simple: We must begin with a commitment never to intentionally kill, or collude in the killing, of any innocent human life, no matter how broken, unformed, disabled or desperate that life may seem. In other words, the choice of certain ways of acting is always and radically incompatible with the love of God and the dignity of the human person created in his image."[9]

The right stuff

"Only tireless promotion of the truth about the human person can infuse democracy with the right values."[10] God will help us acquire the virtues we need for this work in his vineyard. "First and foremost we need the courage and the honesty to speak the truth about human life, no matter how high the cost to ourselves. The great lie of our age is that we are powerless in the face of the compromises, structures and temptations of mass culture. But we are not powerless. We can make a difference. In Christ is our strength and through his grace, we can change the world.

Virtues needed
"We also need the humility to listen well to both friend and opponent on the abortion issue, learning from each and forgetting ourselves. We need the perseverance to continue the struggle for the protection of human life, no matter what the setbacks, trusting in God and in the ultimate fruitfulness of the task he has called us to.

"We need the prudence to know when and how to act in the public arena-and also to recognize and dismiss that fear of acting which postures as prudence itself. And finally we need the great foundation of every apostolic life: faith, hope and charity. Faith not in moral or political abstractions, but in the personal presence of God; hope not in our own ingenuity, but in his goodness and mercy; and love for others, including those who oppose us, rooted in the love God showers down on us."[11]

The public square
We need to bring these virtues with us into the public square where ideas are discussed. This requires some of us to enter the world of politics. True, there are many unpleasant examples of corrupt politicians, and there are also examples of people becoming corrupted once they enter politics. Nevertheless, "we are never to relinquish our participation in public life."[12]

Go into the deep
Sometimes we are tempted to avoid the world because of its bad influences. However, St. Thomas More once said, "Times are never so bad that good people cannot live in them." Indeed, the world was the reason Jesus became man, "For God loved the world so much that he gave his only Son" (Jn 3:16). Therefore we should not be afraid. A wise father once reassured a son who was worried about bringing children into this troubled world, "the world needs more good people like you," he said.

The duties of government towards the family
Decisions made by people holding positions of public authority can have a profound impact on our families. Many families around the world experience difficult relationships with their governments.

"Thus the family, which in God's plan is the basic cell of society and a subject of rights and duties before the State or any other community, finds itself the victim of society, of the delays and slowness with which it acts, and even its blatant injustice. For this reason, the Church openly and strongly defends the rights of the family against the intolerable usurpations of society and the State."[13] "The political community has a duty to honor the family, to assist it, and to ensure especially:
- the freedom to establish a family, have children, and bring them up in keeping with the family's own moral and religious convictions;
- the protection of the stability of the marriage bond and the institution of the family;
- the freedom to profess one's faith, to hand it on, and raise one's children in it, with the necessary means and institutions;
- the right to private property, to free enterprise, to obtain work and housing, and the right to emigrate;
- in keeping with the country's institutions, the right to medical care, assistance for the aged, and family benefits;
- the protection of security and health, especially with respect to dangers like drugs, pornography, alcoholism, etc.;
- the freedom to form associations with other families and so to have representation before civil authority" (*CCC* 2211).

Into all areas of public life
There are many forms of public life outside of politics and public administration; economic, social, and cultural areas desperately need good people too. Therefore, whatever social structure we are in, our "aim should always be the formation of a human person who is cultured, peace-loving, and well disposed towards his fellow men with a view to the benefit of the whole human race."[14]

Oh my God, we're in charge?
There is so much riding on our response to this challenge. What happens here in our nation will affect the rest of the world. "It is primarily U.S. technology, U.S. microchips, U.S. fiber-optics, U.S.

satellites, U.S. habits of thought and entertainment, which are building the neural network of the new global mentality."[15] Knowing that we have such influence should be a sobering thought. It is a challenge we need to take seriously.

We are reminded that "democracy is...a moral adventure, a continuing test of a people's capacity to govern themselves in ways that serve the common good and the good of individual citizens."[16] Because of our freedom we have a choice. We can choose between the road which leads to life, and the road which leads to death (Dt 30:19). The choice is ours to make. It has been said that the future of a nation is decided by every new generation. However in our case, the future of the world is being decided.

Questions

1. What is the significance of the parable of the householder and his vineyard?

   The vineyard is the world, which we are to transform according to the plan of God.

2. Are only those who have taken religious vows supposed to do God's work?

   No. Although the laity and religious have different types of work to do, they have all been called to participate in God's plan.

3. Are the Church and state opposed to each other?

   No. Although the Church and state are autonomous and independent of one another, they are alike in their concern for people, albeit from different vantage points.

4. Why is Christianity important for democratic governments?

   Although the United States is a representative republic, and not a true democracy, a democracy is really nothing more than majority rule. Therefore in order to assure justice and prevent mob rule, citizens must be virtuous. Christianity is necessary for a healthy political community because it upholds the dignity of the human person before utilitarian calculations of productivity and cost-effectiveness.

5. What are the two most threatening attacks upon human life today and why?

   Abortion and euthanasia are most threatening, because they are direct attacks upon human life. Life is the fundamental good without which one cannot enjoy any other right.

Notes

[1] *The Lay Members of Christ's Faithful People,* 40; Gen 1:27.

[2] *Ibid.,* 1.

[3] *Ibid.,* 2.

[4] *Ibid.,* 3.

[5] Second Vatican Ecumenical Council, Dogmatic Constitution on the Church *Lumen Gentium,* 33.

[6] *Living the Gospel of Life: A Challenge to American Catholics,* A Statement from the U.S. Catholic Bishops, 25.

[7] Second Vatican Ecumenical Council, Pastoral Constitution on the Church in the Modern World *Gaudium et Spes,* 76.

[8] *The Lay Members of Christ's Faithful People,* 37.

[9] *Living the Gospel of Life: A Challenge to American Catholics,* A Statement from the U.S. Catholic Bishops, 4.

[10] *Ibid.,* 21.

[11] *Ibid.,* 25.

[12] *Ibid.,* 27.

[13] *The Lay Members of Christ's Faithful People,* 42.

[14] *Familiaris consortio,* 46.

[15] Second Vatican Ecumenical Council, Pastoral Constitution on the Church in the Modern World *Gaudium et Spes,* 74

[16] *Living the Gospel of Life: A Challenge to American Catholics,* A Statement from the U.S. Catholic Bishops, 8.

[17] Ad Limina Remarks to the Bishops of Texas, Oklahoma and Arkansas (June 27, 1998); *Origins* 28:16 (October 1, 1998), 282.

CHAPTER 8

A Different Kind Of Relationship

The sexual relationship is different from all others
We have learned that there are many different kinds of relationships. One of them is very different from all the others. It is a relationship that affects us spiritually, emotionally, physically and also involves a great mystery. The sexual relationship between men and women has always been recognized as pivotal in the lives of individuals and of nations. How we treat it has far reaching effects.

All relationships are built upon communication and sex is no different. It employs the ultimate form of body language. Have you ever heard of body language? Body language is a form of communication that does not involve speech. Rather it communicates our thoughts and feelings through our body. For instance, you can often tell what a person is thinking when you cut them off in traffic. Even though you can't hear them, a picture of their expression is worth a thousand words. Can you think of any other examples of how people can communicate without speaking?

Through the gift of their bodies, a man and a woman express the fullness of their love for one another. They are saying through this gift: "I give myself totally to you – I am yours, you are mine – forever, for keeps." This union of bodies expresses a union of their hearts. Moreover, the joining together of their bodies actually affects their hearts, bringing them closer together emotionally. In short, the two bond together.

Bonding

If bonding is like two pieces of tape sticking together, then breaking up a sexual relationhip is like ripping tape off your arm, except it hurts, much, much worse. Like tape, you leave a piece of yourself behind, and you take a piece of the other person with you. And that is not all, just as tape loses its "stickiness," people lose their ability to bond after multiple sex partners. Studies show that these people are more likely to divorce later on. Many of us have been touched by divorce, and not many of us would say it was a pleasant experience.

In every sexual relationship there is give and take. Love given and taken cannot be undone after a break-up. We are left with less to give our future spouse, and less capacity to receive them. In short, we lose some of our ability to bond.

If done properly, a sexual relationship is like being admitted to the most exclusive country club on earth. A club which has only one member – you. As you may know, the best clubs in town are also the most difficult to join.

A good club won't admit just anybody. An applicant needs to be committed to the club and willing to pay the price before being admitted. Otherwise a club wouldn't be worth joining, would it? The place would be in shambles because nobody would be committed to keeping it up. Rather than taking care of it, we would just as soon move to a club that was in better shape. If anybody could use the place for free, why should we pay? In other words, if your sex were free, why would anyone want to marry you?

Prisoners of love

Have you ever heard of people caught in relationships that were difficult to leave? This happens because they have bonded with the other person emotionally. Even while their mind is telling them to end it, their sexual relationship keeps them together. This occurs most often in abusive relationships, but it can also occur in situations that simply ruin your future plans.

The glue of marriage

Bonding is a very good thing within the context of marriage. A sexual relationship helps a couple grow more deeply in love. In giving themselves to each other they share an intimacy that only they know. The two become one before God and the whole world. Even if the whole world goes crazy, they still have each other and the memories of a shared life.

Royal advice

As a loving father, King Solomon counseled his son about this type of relationship. Keep in mind that Solomon is regarded as the wisest man who ever lived. "Let your fountain be yours alone, not shared with strangers; And have joy of the wife of your youth, your lovely hind, your graceful doe. Her love will invigorate you always, through her love you will flourish continually; When you lie down she will watch over you, and when you wake, she will share your concerns; wherever you turn, she will guide you. Why then, my son, should you go astray for another's wife and accept the embraces of an adulteress? For each man's ways are plain to the Lord's sight; all their paths he surveys; By his own iniquities the wicked man will be caught, in the meshes of his own sin he will be held fast; He will die from lack of discipline, through the greatness of his folly he will be lost" (Prv 5:17-23).

Why risk being divorced? Why risk losing a relationship with someone who will always be there for us, someone who will be concerned and watching over us – a person who shares our interests and makes us number one in his or her life? That is what we are doing when we sleep around. As King Solomon told his son, this is a stupid thing to do.

What is your E.Q.?

Psychologists agree that high I.Q. does not necessarily predict who will succeed in life. They agree that I.Q. contributes only about 20 percent of the factors that determine success. Some researchers recently set out to discover why so many intelligent people grow up unhappy and unsuccessful. They concluded that E.Q. or emotional quotient was a greater determinant of success than I.Q.[1] An important element of E.Q. is impulse control. The essence of this emotional self-regulation is the ability to delay impulse in the service of a goal.

To begin their study they visited preschool students and gave them each a marshmallow. They then promised them a second marshmallow if they would wait until the researchers returned before eating it. When the researchers returned twenty minutes later, some had already eaten their marshmallows, but some had waited. The researchers then followed these children to adulthood.

What do you think they found? They found that the ones who had waited before eating the first marshmallow grew up happier and more successful than those who did not wait. This concluded that this aptitude for making the best choice was far more beneficial than mere intelligence. This was what King Solomon was trying to teach his son. Surely the son of a king could have had anything he wanted - whenever he wanted. But as they say, timing is everything.

Real love

Just as timing is important, so is commitment. Love is more than a feeling. Feelings come and go with the weather. But true love is a commitment, an act of the will. St. John Chrysostom suggests that young husbands say this to their wives: "I have taken you in my arms, and I love you, and I prefer you to my life itself. For the present life is nothing, and my most ardent dream is to spend it with you in such a way that we may be assured of not being separated in the life reserved for us....I place your love above all things, and nothing would be more bitter or painful to me than to be of a different mind than you" (*CCC* 2365).

Real love can save your life

While it is clear that sex affects us emotionally, there is another benefit to marriage – good health. A faithful marriage can save your life. We have all heard of sexually transmitted diseases, but have you heard that we are living in the middle of an epidemic? It's true. The number of sexually transmitted diseases is on the increase. Many of these are painful and disfiguring. Some can even make you sterile and incapable of having children. Others you don't even know you have until it is too late. Some are incurable, and some can even kill you.

Condoms aren't the solution. They aren't totally effective in preventing pregnancy, nor do they stop the AIDS virus. The AIDS virus is so small that it passes right through the natural holes found in latex condoms. Condoms also don't protect the spread of disease from skin-to-skin contact; you can catch some awful stuff on your abdomen, legs and other places.

These frightening statistics are not faceless. They involve good kids. Kids just like you who thought they could take chances. They thought it would never happen to them because they were with a "good" person too. Well, this epidemic did not get started by people who infected themselves on purpose. They all thought they were safe, or at least safe enough. They were wrong. Some were dead wrong.

Think of it this way. Having sex with somebody is like having sex with every person your partner has ever been with. Former partners not only left a piece of themselves behind emotionally; they may also have left behind a contagious virus, bacteria, fungus, or parasite. Looks can be deceiving. Just because the other person looks clean and has a good reputation doesn't mean you're safe. That person could have done something stupid once before, and is about to do so again. It only takes once.

Questions

1. What message does sex communicate to the persons involved?
   Sex is a form of body language that conveys the message, "I give myself totally to you – I am yours, you are mine – forever, for keeps."

2. How does sex effect people emotionally?
   Two people in a sexual relationship bond together emotionally. The closeness of their bodies mirrors the closeness of their hearts.

3. Why do multiple sexual relationships increase the likelihood of divorce?
   Multiple sexual relationships decrease a person's ability to bond when they marry, and may increase their chances of divorce.

4. How can a faithful marriage save your life?
   A faithful marriage allows for only one sexual relationship. Multiple sexual partners increase the chances of catching sexually transmitted diseases, some of which are fatal.

Notes
[1] Daniel Goleman, Ph.D., *Emotional Intelligence.*

CHAPTER 9

A Great Mystery

Sex is the beginning of life

As we have discussed, sex affects us spiritually, emotionally, and physically. However, there is much, much more to it than that. Sex involves a great mystery. It is the beginning of another person's life. It is a relationship where 1+1=3. When the father's sperm meets the mother's egg, an explosion of life occurs. A new person comes into existence. This same person will exist for all eternity. The *Catechism* reminds us of its significance: "Let all be convinced that human life ... is not limited to the horizons of this life only: its true evaluation and full significance can be understood only in reference to man's eternal destiny" (*CCC* 2371).

Our awesome power

Our sexual power is our greatest power. Through it we have a share in God's creative action. The reality of this underscores the importance of a sexual relationship. We change the universe forever by bringing into existence another human being who did not exist before and who will exist for all eternity. Not just any human being, but a person just like us – our child.

That is why sex is such a big deal. If it involved nothing more than a good time (like some television shows would lead us to believe) then nobody would talk much about it. But people *do* recognize its significance. Why do you think the juiciest gossip stories always involve sex? We recognize to some degree that this is a big deal. Sexual relationships have always been important to individuals and to communities for a variety of reasons.

It's never an accident
Pregnancy is never an accident. It only occurs after sex. It doesn't occur because of handshakes or kisses or any other natural activity. It occurs when a man and woman give themselves to one another sexually. Therefore it follows that if sex is chosen, then so is the possibility of a child. That is simply how we are made. The only accident is misunderstanding the deep significance of this relationship.

Of course pregnancy does not always occur. And there are also artificial ways in which people try to manipulate the outcome, but we will save that for the next chapter. For now, it is important to understand that by having sex, we are doing everything in our power to become a parent. What more could we possibly do?

It all adds up
The love between mother and father sets off an unseen chain reaction. The explosion of life occurs the split second a sperm cell burrows its way into the mother's egg (ovum). In that instant an entirely new, and different genetic human constitution is created. The 23 chromosomes from the father join the 23 chromosomes of the mother. Together they constitute the 46 chromosomes of another human being with a unique DNA pattern. All of this extremely complex biology is set in motion by our choice to have sex. Once we do it, the results are out of our control. It is like diving into a pool. Once we jump, gravity takes over. There is no turning back.

This fertilized egg is now a living human being. All the genetic information that a person will ever need is now present. For example, the child's sex, eye and hair color, height, and so on are all determined. Moreover, the child is fully human. Dr. Jerome Lejeune, a world-renowned geneticist testified: "I would call it human because I know that the whole [genetic] information is human. I can read it. I can see the dimensions and make up of the chromosomes....I know by its own information that it will develop itself. It just needs nurture and protection."[1]

Whether a person is one minute old or one hundred years old, the 4 Principles of Life apply equally to both of them. Do you remember what these principles are?

We depend on one another

Have you ever seen pictures of a child developing in its mother's womb? You know the ones that begin by showing the fertilized egg as a dot, then progressing every month until birth? Aren't you struck by how humble our beginnings are, and how much we depended on others for life? Some would say that we remain dependent on others. We are not as independent as we sometimes think. For example, we need help in fixing our cars and computers, don't we? We should remind ourselves of this the next time we get too cocky. It is easy to think more of ourselves than we ought to.

An eyewitness account

Another striking thing about our development is how quietly our lives started. In most cases we were alive and growing before our mothers even knew about it. Kids are sneaky, aren't they? Check out this remarkable testimony given by Dr. Paul E. Rockwell:

"Eleven years ago while giving an anesthetic for a ruptured ectopic pregnancy (at two months gestation) I was handed what I believe was the smallest living human being ever seen. The embryo sac was intact and transparent. Within the sac was a tiny (approx. 1 cm.) human male swimming extremely vigorously in the amniotic fluid, while attached to the wall by the umbilical cord. This tiny human was perfectly developed, with long, tapering fingers, feet and toes. It was almost transparent, as regards the skin, and the delicate arteries and veins were prominent to the ends of the fingers.

"The baby was extremely alive and swam about the sac approximately one time per second, with a natural swimmer's stroke. This tiny human did not look at all like the photos and drawings and models of 'embryos' which I have seen, nor did it look like a few embryos I have been able to observe since then, obviously because this one was alive!...when the sac was opened, the tiny human immediately lost its life and took on the appearance of what is accepted as the appearance of an embryo at this age"[2]

One mother's courage

Even though our lives started in secret we were never alone. God was with us from the beginning. The brave Jewish mother whose seven sons were martyred acknowledged this when she encouraged them: "I do not know how you came into existence in my womb; It was not I who gave you the breath of life, nor was it I who set in order the elements of which each of you is composed. Therefore since it is the Creator of the universe, who shapes each man's beginning, as he brings about the origin of everything, he, in his mercy, will give you back both breath and life, because you now disregard yourselves for the sake of his law" (2 Mc 7:22-23).

What does the Bible say?

The Bible speaks often of God's intervention in the womb: "you formed my inmost being; you knit me in my mother's womb. I praise you, so wonderfully you made me; wonderful are your works! My very self you knew; my bones were not hidden from you, when I was being made in secret, fashioned as in the depths of the earth. Your eyes foresaw my actions; in your book all are written down; my days were shaped, before one came to be" (Ps 139:13-16).

"Before I formed you in the womb I knew you, before you were born I dedicated you" (Jer 1:5).[3]

What impresses you about these passages? How do these impressions compare to your impressions regarding genetic science? Scripture sees conception as being of divine origin rather than human. In light of all we know of genetics how can this be so?

God creates, we cooperate

Sex means marriage. Remember what we said about sex being the ultimate form of body language? It means I give myself totally to you. It may even mean I want to have a baby. But conception doesn't automatically follow. This aspect of sex is beyond our control. We cannot will creation, simply because we cannot will the activity of our egg or sperm. They operate independently of us according to the nature given them by the Creator. Moreover, only God can create a spiritual soul; egg and sperm are matter without souls of their own. Couples can only will to give themselves to each other.

Even with all our technological advances we must acknowledge that God is ultimately in control, just as the people in the Old Testament believed. The interaction of our wills, the complexity of our natures, and the purposes of God are reasons why the beginning of life remains an awesome mystery.

Questions

1. When does human life begin?

Human life begins when the father's sperm meets the mother's egg. The 23 chromosomes from the father join the 23 chromosomes from the mother. Together they constitute the 46 chromosomes of another human being with a unique DNA pattern.

2. How do the sperm and egg get together?

Ask your parents.

3. How come we call God the Creator?

We call God the Creator because only he can create a new immortal soul. Moreover he designed the natures by which we bring new life into the world. Through our actions, God invites us to participate in his act of creation.

Notes

[1] Expert testimony rendered during *New Jersey v. Alexander Loce et. als.* 1991.

[2] National Catholic Conference of Bishops, United States Catholic Conference, *Documentation on the Right to Life and Abortion,* 1974.

[3] See also, Is 44:2,24.

CHAPTER 10

The Marriage Relationship

Marriage makes a sexual relationship good

As a diver ascends the highest platform, she looks like the loneliest person on earth. High above the crowd she stands alone with her thoughts. What do you suppose she is feeling before her dive? Probably a little fear, which isn't all bad, because fear makes us alert. Hopefully she is also thinking of how she will execute the dive safely, and with style. For to be a good diver you not only have to survive, but you have got to look good doing it.

This sounds a lot like love, doesn't it? To a man and woman in love the world can seem like a far-away place. They can have their "head in the clouds" as they think of nothing but their beloved. They may feel a rush of powerful emotions overtake them. And like divers, they too will return to the ground. However, for lovers to do this safely and with style, they will have to follow the principles of good relationships, which is showing love in an appropriate way.

As we discussed in the last chapter babies are the natural outcome of sex. This must be assumed, just as divers assume there is water in the pool. If we are not ready to be a parent, we are not ready for sex. Marriage is to the lover what water is to the diver. Without it we are setting ourselves up for a hard fall. We are also doing the same for our child.

A safe landing

Marriage gives children the stable family structure they need. Anything less than this arrangement is second best, and may even be disastrous. It is true that many people are adopted or live in single-parent homes; some children are even raised by grandparents or guardians. Nevertheless, even these heroic people will agree that a good marriage between biological parents is the best family arrangement of all.

Marriage is not only good for children; it is also good for us. It alone can give us the complete package of emotional and physical security we need. It gives us confidence in mutual love and support, and also in physical health. This is because marital love is exclusive and not shared with anyone else. It is also a lifelong commitment that is made freely. It is based on a decision to love, not on "feelings" alone.

"I do" vs. "I might"
What confidence would you have in a promise that was only kept as long as the other person felt like it? What incentive would you have to devote the best years of your life to someone if they were free to leave you whenever they felt like it? Such a relationship would not be very real. We are fickle. Our emotions are constantly changing. They depend on a lot of things that are outside of our control – like the weather for instance. The point is this: a commitment based on feelings alone is no commitment at all.

Sure, feelings play a big part in bringing couples together, and even keeping them together. But marriage is about keeping our promises to one another. These promises are called marriage vows. "The intimate union of marriage, as a mutual giving of two persons… demands total fidelity from the spouses and requires an unbreakable union between them" (*CCC* 1646). This "oneness" is God's purpose for marriage (Gn 2:24). It is compared to the mystical union of Christ and his Church (Eph 5:23-33). Marriage is the closest relationship anyone can enjoy in this world.

The solemn commitment of marriage can be difficult to make - and keep. It can even be a little scary like a high-dive. Nevertheless, we can be confident in the Lord's blessing. "This covenant between baptized persons has been raised by Christ the Lord to the dignity of a sacrament" (*CCC* 1601). Indeed, God himself is the author of marriage (*CCC* 1603). He wants us to succeed.

Helping each other get to heaven
Spouses also get help from one another - not only in marriage, but also in getting to heaven. "For this reason a man shall leave his father and his mother and be joined to his wife, and the two shall become one flesh. This is a great mystery, but I speak in reference to Christ and the Church" (Eph 5:31-32). Wow! Marriage is somehow linked to God's plan of salvation. While we won't plumb the depths of that mystery here, we will note that marriage is profoundly significant.

Because of this significance, it is good to marry someone who shares our faith. Through it we have the example of the Holy Family of Jesus, Mary and Joseph, and the knowledge that human marriage mirrors the love between the Father and Son from which the Holy Spirit proceeds. Practically speaking, it is reassuring to know that our spouse shares our mind in loving and serving God, and that we will be in agreement on the faith we teach our children. This may not seem so important during courtship, but that will change when we begin living our lives together.

Therefore it is important for our spouse to understand the full significance of marriage and family life. Would it be reasonable for two Olympic pairs skaters to have two different trainers telling them two different things? Not only would it be ugly to watch, but it could be dangerous as well. Helping each other get to heaven is one of a couple's biggest responsibilities. Without a shared faith, couples can expect a few skates in the face, and a few drops along the way.

Viva la difference
Have you ever been at a gathering where everyone was either all male or all female? For example, have you ever been in an assembly at an all-girls or all-boys school? Or been around a girls' or boys' team? It is different isn't it? You especially notice it if you are of the opposite sex. There is something different about it; not necessarily good or bad, just different.

This difference is good. God made us both male and female (Gn 1:27), God is the source of our sexuality. He made the two sexes for each other. The Bible says: "it is not good for the man to be alone" (Gn 2:18). The woman is "flesh of his flesh," i.e., his counterpart, his equal, his nearest in all things, given to him by God as a "helpmate" (*CCC* 1605).

The love between husband and wife is an image of the love God has for all of us. This love is good, very good, in the Creator's eyes. And this love which God blesses is intended to be fruitful (*CCC* 1604). The Bible says God blessed Adam and Eve and said to them, "Be fertile and multiply; fill the earth and subdue it" (Gn 1:28). Notice that God said this to Adam and Eve as a couple, not as individuals. Marriage must come first, because it is necessary for the proper nurture and protection of children. A mother and father complement one another in the performance of this vital task. While being equal co-heirs of the kingdom of God, they have different gifts. These gifts are necessary for a child to develop to his full emotional and physical potential.

The gift of fertility
Men and women also differ in their fertility. Men are always fertile, while women are fertile for only a short period of time each month. A woman's cyclical fertility will conclude at menopause, while a man's remains fertile until death. In this way the two complement each other in the execution of God's plan for our lives. "It is good to keep in mind that fertility is a great good: to be fertile is a state of health for an adult person. It is those among us who are not fertile who need to be helped and who seek treatment for infertility. Women now take a pill to thwart their fertility, as if fertility were a disease against which we need a cure. Contraception treats the women's body as if there were something wrong with it. The use of contraception suggests God made a mistake in the way that He designed the body and that we must correct His error.

"In an age where we have become very wary of dumping pollutants into the environment, it is ironic that we are so willing to dump pollutants into our bodies. The health risks of contraception are considerable – take a look at the insert pages in any package of the pill."[1]

Did you know that when they where first testing the contraceptive pill, they were also testing one for men? It is true. However, there were some complications. It seems that some of the women died, while some of the men experienced shrinkage of their testicles. How did the researchers react? They discontinued the male pill and lowered the dosage of the female pill. Obviously this doesn't show women very much respect. Today women continue to die, and they suffer other side-effects as well.[2]

A mission that is not impossible

Fertility is a gift. A child does not come from outside as something added on to the mutual love of the spouses, but springs from the very heart of that mutual giving, as its fruit and fulfillment. Called to give life, spouses share in the creative power and fatherhood of God (*CCC* 2366-2367).

Married couples should be fully aware of their mission of responsible parenthood. This requires that spouses recognize their duties toward God, toward themselves, toward the family, and toward human society, as they maintain a correct set of priorities.[3] There are many ways in which to prioritize. Why would you think this order is best?

There are many individuals and groups opposed to new life. They think that the fewer children the better. People will often say hurtful things to parents who have more than one or two children. They have been known to say such silly things as, "How are you going to send them all to college?" They say this as if you actually needed a degree to get into Heaven. A college education is good, but it probably wasn't on God's mind when he told Adam and Eve to "Have many children, so that your descendents will live all over the earth and bring it under their control" (Gn 1:28).

God is the Creator of life, and therefore also of families. He is the one who designed the generation of new life. He knows better than anyone how all of this fits together. In light of this, don't you think God's plan should be the priority here? Who knows better than he how marriage is supposed to work? Wouldn't you trust a certified mechanic to fix your Corvette before your family doctor? Okay, a Ford Escort may be a more realistic example. But the point is that God wants us to have a "high-performance" marriage and he's the one who knows how we can get it. He wants us to have relationships that are true, beautiful and good.

"Your mission if you choose to accept it is…"

The Church teaches us that there is an unbreakable connection between the unitive meaning and the procreative meaning of sex. "This connection was established by God, and man is not permitted to break it through his own volition."[4] This is the only way for a sexual relationship to be true, beautiful and good. God's plan for sex is that it be open to life, and that babies should only come from a sexual relationship between a man and woman who are married to each other. In other words, sex must be open to life and open to love.

Therefore such things as creating babies in a laboratory, contraception, masturbation and homosexual acts are wrong because they don't fulfill this dual requirement of God's plan for human happiness. Granted there are many surrounding circumstances that might help explain such behavior, but such behavior can never be justified. This might sound obvious, but in recent years this has become obscured. Many have tried to "modify" God's plan. Contraception is just one example.

One of the problems with contraception is that it undercuts the procreative aspect of sex. By withholding our fertility we are not open to life; we are against it, that's what "contra" means. This withholding violates the unitive aspect of sex as well. Your body says, "I give myself totally to you" while contracepting holds back. It is like saying one thing and then doing another. This is a contradiction, and any contradiction cannot be true. You cannot give yourself, and not-give yourself at the same time. Contraception is wrong because it "leads not only to a positive refusal to be open to life but also to a falsification of the inner truth of conjugal love (married sexual love)" (*CCC* 2370).

Questions

1. Why is marriage the only right situation for a sexual relationship?
   Marriage is the only right situation for a sexual relationship because the couple's commitment to each other provides a stable environment for themselves and for their children.

2. Why is it prudent to marry someone who shares our faith?
   It is prudent to marry someone who shares our faith because it increases your chances of agreeing on important matters such as raising children. However, this is not to say that you must do so.

3. Are men and women different? Why?
   Men and women are different in the sense that they are complementary. Together they mirror the glory of God, and fulfill his plan for creation.

4. Why is contraception wrong?
   Contraception is wrong because it leads to a refusal to be open to life, and also because it prevents a total giving between the spouses. It is God's plan for sex to be both procreative and unitive, and exclusively within marriage.

Notes

[1] Prof. Janet Smith, *Humanae Vitae: A Challenge to Love*, p.11.
[2] Dr. Ellen Grant, *The Bitter Pill*, p.19.
[3] *Humanae Vitae*, 10.
[4] *Ibid.*, 12.

CHAPTER 11

God Always Forgives.
People Sometimes Forgive.
Nature Never Forgives.

Our actions have consequences

We all want our mistakes to be as small, inexpensive and as short-lived as possible. For example, if we are going to be penalized in a ballgame, we don't want it to be the deciding factor between winning and losing. We would want an opportunity to undo our mistake, and to make amends for our failure. In short, we would want to be forgiven.

We feel the same way off the field too. The Bible tells us that we have all sinned by failing to obey God's law (1 Jn 1:8). Sin hurts our relationship with God. Not only does this make us unhappy, God isn't happy about it either. He loves us so much that he doesn't want anything to come between us and him. That is why he sent Jesus to restore our friendship with him (Jn 3:16; Mt 9:5).

God always forgives

To accomplish this, God gave us the wonderful Sacrament of Reconciliation, which is sometimes known as Confession. Through this sacrament we receive his forgiveness for the sins which have hurt our relationship with him. We also receive the grace to be stronger the next time we are tempted. The Bible says, "if we acknowledge our sins, he is faithful and just and will forgive our sins and cleanse us from every wrongdoing" (1Jn 1:9).

Going to Confession is a humbling experience. Like fasting, it makes us less self-centered. It forces us to recognize God as Creator and Lord. We come face to face with our own humanity, and the fact that we are not the center of the universe. Wise people know this is a healthy disposition to have. A famous intellectual once mocked another famous intellectual for becoming a Catholic. He scoffed at the idea of seeing his friend kneeling in a confessional. To which the new convert replied, "I never feel taller than when I am on my knees." What do you think he meant by that?

People sometimes forgive
Unlike God, people forgive imperfectly. Even though God wants us to forgive one another, it doesn't always happen. Adam and Eve's sin left us all with an inclination towards evil. Since everyone is at varying degrees of spiritual maturity in overcoming their sinful habits, the quality of forgiveness will vary from person to person. Many people do not even forgive at all. For them it is "an eye for an eye." Meaning that if you do something to them, they will do the same to you.

Nature never forgives
Losing the friendship of God and of others is not the only consequence of sin. We still suffer from our sinful actions even after God has forgiven us. "The forgiveness of sin and restoration of communion with God entail the remission of the eternal punishment of sin, but temporal punishment remains. This punishment must not be conceived of as a kind of vengeance inflicted by God from without, but as following from the very nature of sin" (CCC 1472).

The Natural Law
The negative consequences attached to disobeying God are due to not treating things according to their natures. Nature being defined as that which makes something what it is, as distinct from something else. It is the defining characteristics and behavior of a particular reality. When we fail to treat things according to their natures, we break the Natural Law, which is a participation in Divine Law. It is that part of God's law we can discover by reason alone without God revealing it to us.

"For example, suppose you see your friend Freddy, with the hood of his car up, holding a can of oil in one hand and a can of molasses in the other, and you ask, 'What are you doing?' Freddy answers, 'Trying to decide whether to put oil or molasses in my car.' If you were a real friend of Freddy, how would you respond? Would you say 'Freddy, how do you feel about it?' No, you would say, 'Freddy, you should do good by your car. And the good is that which is in accord with the nature of the thing. Oil is good for cars. Molasses isn't.' 'Yeah, but this is a Chevy.' 'Freddy, it doesn't make any difference. Cars are all the same.' 'Is that right? Well, who are you to tell me what to do with my car?' 'If you don't believe me, Freddy, look in the glove compartment at the manufacturer's directions.' (This is, by analogy, what the Natural Law and the Ten Commandments are – a set of manufacturer's directions.) So Freddy looks at the owner's manual and sees, in red letters on page 10, 'Use oil – do not use molasses.' Freddy says, 'That's what it says all right. But wait a minute. Whose car is this? It's my car. [It's my body, etc.] They can't push me around. I'll do what I want with my car.' So Freddy puts in the molasses. He is sincere. He is liberated. He is pro-choice. And he is a pedestrian. Why? Because, whether we are talking about automobiles, human beings, or society, the natural law is the story of how things work."[1]

Babies are a natural occurrence
Pregnancy is an example of a natural result following certain behavior. In most cases it is a reason to celebrate, but for people not ready to be parents it is a big problem. Contrary to modern opinion, abortion is never a solution because it cannot undo the fact that the child exists. Moreover, a child in its mother's womb is made in the image of God, sacred, valuable and a part of God's plan – just as we are. Remember the 4 Principles of Life? And like other violations of the Natural Law, there are often grave consequences attached.

Protecting life is a duty
The Natural Law does not depend on Divine Revelation to be known. There are some things that we are able to figure out on our own, and preventing murder is one of them. Even if God had never forbidden it, it still would have been necessary to make murder illegal. Otherwise we wouldn't be able to live together; it is only logical.

Nevertheless, because it is important, God does forbid murder, which applies to abortion as well. "Although Sacred Scripture never addresses the question of deliberate abortion…they show such great respect for the human being in the mother's womb that it requires as a logical consequence that God's commandment 'You shall not kill' be extended to the unborn child as well (Ex 20:13).

"This has been the teaching of the Church throughout Christianity's two thousand year history. From its first contacts with the Greco-Roman world, where abortion and infanticide were widely practiced, the first Christian community, by its teaching and practice, radically opposed the customs rampant in that society."[2] More recently, the Second Vatican Council defines abortion as an "unspeakable crime."[3]

Nature cannot forgive

Now just as Freddy in the above example chose to pour molasses into his car, people choose to participate in abortion. And like Freddy they can never undo what they have done. Even though God forgives us, and people may forgive us, we still must live with the natural consequences of our actions. No amount of contrition can undo the damage. It doesn't matter how many times you tell your father "sorry" for smashing up his car, or how many times he says "I forgive you." The car is still a wreck and you feel terrible about it. You cannot turn back the hands of time. What's done is done. You have to live with it. It is in this sense that nature is unforgiving. This is not to say that God never intervenes, but that there is a natural order to things that must be respected.

The consequences of abortion

A thing is not wrong simply because there are bad consequences attached to it. For example, abortion is wrong because it is unjust, not just because there are bad side effects. Nevertheless, bad behavior often does have bad consequences attached to it and abortion is no exception. It is a huge tragedy that has hurt millions of people. First and foremost it hurts the child. We won't get into the details of an actual abortion in this book, but for those who think it is no big deal, you owe it to yourself to be better informed. Take some time to research what the various abortion procedures actually do to the poor children.

It may sound strange, but abortion also hurts the parents who chose it in the first place. Whether they are surgical or chemical, abortions can have serious physical complications. These often go unreported in abortion clinic statistics because the injured women are admitted to hospitals, which then assume the responsibility for their care. Some common adverse physical effects include: sterility, future miscarriages and ectopic pregnancies, bleeding, perforated uterus, blood clots and death. Just to name a few.

Post-abortion syndrome
Recent medical studies have also observed and identified serious
emotional and psychological complications following abortion.
Often referred to as Post-Abortion Syndrome (PAS), its symptoms
can appear many years after the abortion. PAS occurs when parents
deny the natural grief they feel due to the loss of their unborn child.

Here is a short sampling of PAS symptoms: grief, denial, guilt,
emptiness, nightmares, anger, eating disorders, shame, depression,
panic attacks, sexual dysfunction, loss of self-esteem, broken relationships, desire for a replacement child, coldness toward children,
being overly interested in babies, etc. Somehow abortions also seem
to destroy the relationship between the parents. This list could continue, but you get the idea. The good news is that there is professional help available to assist us in the healing process.[4]

Real people, true stories
The statistics of abortion are so overwhelming that we sometimes
forget the individual tragedies connected with each of them.
Annually in the United States approximately 1.4 million abortions
leave one person dead and two wounded. The child dies, and its parents usually survive, though wounded by the experience. One such
couple is Pete and Barbara Metzelaars. You may remember Pete from
his many years as the star tight end for the Buffalo Bills professional
football team. Even though he and Barbara enjoyed fabulous success
on the field, off the field their lives felt incomplete because of an
abortion they chose when they were younger.

"We didn't know where to turn. We thought having an abortion was
the only alternative. We didn't know all the facts," says Barbara.
"Although I have forgiveness in Christ, my heart aches each day
thinking about our baby. I wonder what my baby would have
looked like, what he would be like, would he have precious little
hands and feet like other babies..?" Pete and Barbara would give anything to have their child back.

It seems that abortion was not the solution to their problem. They
cannot undo the fact that the child existed. Today they warn others
about the illusion of choice. As Barbara says, "All the abortion
providers want is your money, they won't be there to help you deal
with the pain afterwards." Later they struck up a friendship with

another Buffalo Bills couple, Mark and Robin Kelso. They discovered that Mark and Robin counseled young people considering abortion. In doing so they offered real choices; choices that made the best of a difficult situation, not ones that made it worse.

Pete and Barbara wish they had met the Kelsos earlier. They didn't know that there are thousands of places around the country that offer positive alternatives to abortion. To find one, just look in the phone book yellow pages under Abortion Alternatives, or perhaps Clinics.

Real men do cry
We can be tempted to think that PAS occurs only in women, but men are affected as well. Even though they are generally better at avoiding their post-abortion feelings, men still suffer because of it. They come to realize that the women and children were victims of their irresponsibility. They realize that they took the easy way out by telling the woman that they would support her "choice." When the women may rather have heard that he was willing to take care of her and her baby.

Friends and parents often make the same mistake. Instead of suggesting positive alternatives like adoption, they think they are being heroic in supporting an abortion. They forget that the mother already has a relationship with her child, and that anything that hurts the child will hurt the mother.

Different expectations
For a woman, a man's willingness to abort their child is an indication that their relationship isn't strong; he doesn't love her enough to have their baby. This is a terrible time to discover that "I want to have sex with you," isn't the same thing as saying, "I want to have a baby with you." It is the difference between taking-love and giving-love.

This reflects another important difference between men and women. There is an old saying, "Women play at sex to get love, while men play at love to get sex." Generally speaking, it means that men and women have two very different expectations of sex. Even if the expectations were reversed, it would still be true that they weren't "on the same page." The best way to protect the expectations of each is through a commitment of marriage before they have sex. The acceptance of abortion has fueled male irresponsibility, because they can now get off the hook for just a couple hundred dollars.

Helpless fathers

On the other hand, men can be denied any role in caring for the woman and child. They have no rights. Try as they might, they have no legal standing to prevent the killing of their unborn children. If the woman chooses it, it is all over for the child. Many men live with the pain, and regret having a sexual relationship with the wrong woman.

Corrupts society

Other people involved in an abortion include grandparents, relatives, friends, doctors, nurses, lawmakers, judges – anybody directly or indirectly involved in facilitating its practice. Abortion corrupts our systems of medicine and justice by turning things on their head. Medicine is now used to harm as well as heal, and the law is used to justify what is unjust, namely the killing of an innocent person. This is a disturbing development that has grave implications for the future of human rights. Why do you think this is so? Can you think of any historical parallels where human rights were denied? What were the reasons given to justify their denial?

Abortion also affects those who are deprived of a relationship they might otherwise have had with the child, such as brothers and sisters, extended family, the Church, the community, etc. Abortion affects people we may never have even considered. Mother Teresa was once asked why God hadn't sent us someone to cure AIDS. She responded that he did, but that we had aborted him. We must remember that we are social beings, and that we have a relationship with our children even if they have yet to leave their mother's womb.

A word of hope and healing

Pope John Paul II has a word of hope and healing for women hurting from abortion, "I would now like to say a special word to women who have had an abortion. The church is aware of the many factors, which may have influenced your decision, and she does not doubt that in many cases it was a painful and even shattering decision. The wound in your heart may not yet have healed. Certainly what happened was and remains terribly wrong. But do not give in to discouragement and do not lose hope.

"Try rather to understand what happened and face it honestly. If you have not already done so, give yourselves over with humility and trust to repentance. The Father of mercies is ready to give you his forgiveness and his peace in the Sacrament of Reconciliation. You will come to understand that nothing is definitively lost and you will also be able to ask forgiveness from your child, who is now living in the Lord. With the friendly and expert advice of other people, and as a result of your own painful experience, you can be among the most eloquent defenders of everyone's right to life."[5]

Questions

1. Is everyone a sinner?
   The Bible says that all have sinned by failing to obey God's law
   (1John 1:8).

2. How can we be reconciled to God?
   We can be reconciled to God through the sacrament of
   Reconciliation. Acting in the person of Jesus Christ, the priest
   has the power to absolve us from our sins and give us the grace
   to avoid sin in the future.

3. What is the Natural Law?
   The natural law is a participation in the divine law. It is that part
   of God's law we can discover by reason alone without God
   revealing it to us.

4. How can we know abortion is wrong?
   We can know abortion is wrong through both the natural law
   and divine revelation. Naturally, we know that killing should be
   banned because we will not be able to live together if we don't.
   Moreover, God proscribed killing with the Fifth Commandment,
   "Thou Shall Not Kill" (Ex 20:13).

5. If a girl gets pregnant, does it mean the guy will marry her?
   "I want to have sex with you," is much different from "I want to
   have a baby with you." The first is an example of taking-love,
   and the second is an example of giving-love. Although his body is
   communicating self-giving, his motives may simply be that of
   taking pleasure at the girl's expense. Therefore, a guy may not
   marry a girl simply because he got her pregnant.

6. If a guy gets a girl pregnant, can he take care of the baby if he
   wants to?
   A man who is not married to the mother of his child has no legal
   rights over that child. The mother could abort the baby even if
   the father wants to keep him or her.

Notes

[1] Prof. Charles E. Rice, *50 Questions on the Natural Law,* p. 203.

[2] *Gospel of Life,* 61.

[3] *Guadium et Spes,* 51.

[4] For more on the physical and emotional consequences of abortion, see: www.marquette.edu/rachel, www.ramahinternational.org, www.afterabortion.org.

[5] *Gospel of Life,* 99.

CHAPTER 12

Do Not Be Afraid

We can trust God even with our sexuality

Life is filled with uncertainty. We never know what will be thrown at us next. However, we do know that if we follow good principles, we will be able to handle most anything that comes our way. Whether it is a curveball or a fastball, a hitter must keep his eye on the ball if he hopes to hit it. So too, we must follow good principles in our relationships if we wish to be happy.

And, just like in baseball, people are temped to cheat in their relationships. Cheating relationships may seem good, but they really are not. They may make us happy for a moment, but in the long run we are worse off.

Cheating is often caused by fear. For example, we cheat in sports because we are afraid of losing. Instead of persevering under pressure, we lose our nerve and take a shortcut. Even though we may think we are taking the only "reasonable" alternative, we are in fact risking everything. Being afraid causes much evil. Remember our discussion on the ends justifying the means? This is something we should never do.

We tend to rationalize our bad relationships. We make excuses for our cheating. Many of us have said: "I am a pretty good person. I know I do things I shouldn't do, but you should see what so and so does." Sound familiar? This is like a high jumper lowering the bar to avoid failure. We deceive ourselves when we compare ourselves to others. This is the wrong standard of measure. Just as winning the

High Jump requires clearing the bar at its highest point, so too does happiness depend upon our living by the high standards of good relationships.

Fear causes us to lower our personal standards. Make a list of reasons people give for being sexually active outside of marriage. Which of these are motivated by fear?

The overpopulation hoax
Fear is also a contributing factor to the practice of contraception. Many years ago, certain people were predicting that we would run out of natural resources because the world was over populated. They also said that this scarcity would cause global war. Therefore, in order to avoid poverty and war, we had to lower the population. The chief means proposed for accomplishing this were contraception, sterilization, and abortion.

Time has proven the population doomsayers wrong. In fact, many populations are shrinking. They are not even replacing the people who die each year. And contrary to predictions, countries with growing populations are also experiencing growing economies. It appears that people produce much more than they eat (although your parents may disagree).

Our purpose here is not to study population demographics, but rather to point out that we were frightened into doing something that was wrong. Something that we might not have done otherwise. The tragic consequences of contraception were foreseen by a few, and their predictions did come true.

One of the predictions was that governments would interfere with family life once contraception was accepted.[1] Today this prediction has become a horrible reality. In countries like China people who have more than one child are forcibly aborted and sterilized. Here in the West the size of our families is still voluntary.

Nevertheless many people will make insensitive remarks and ask invasive questions if you have any more than just a couple of children. They say things like: "Aren't you finished yet?" "There are ways to fix that, don't you know?" or "Why don't you go to the vet and get yourself fixed?" They say it as if it were clever to compare you to a dog. In China it isn't a laughing matter.

The high cost of cowardice

Many believed that abortion was needed as a backup for failed contraception. Without it they thought a whole host of evils would descend upon society. Once again, we were frightened into accepting something we knew was wrong. By the time people realized it was killing, they had already gotten used to it. In other words, now that it can be proven that abortion kills an innocent human being, people no longer care.

This sounds like the frog in the pot story. If you put a frog in boiling water it will jump out. But if you raise the temperature slowly, it will happily stay in the pot until it is cooked. Sadly, there is a lot of frog in all of us. Simply knowing something is wrong is not enough. We have to want to do the right thing. Mother Teresa of Calcutta said that abortion would be with us until we learned to love. Until then, it looks like we will remain in the pot.

The advancing culture of death

This failure to love has brought us to the brink of yet another disaster – Euthanasia. Through contraception and abortion we try to control the beginning of life. Through euthanasia we try to control the end of life. In both cases, we make ourselves out to be God. We want to take control of death and bring it about before its time, 'gently' ending one's own life or the life of others. In reality, what might seem logical and humane, when looked at more closely, is seen to be senseless and inhumane.

"Here we are faced with one of the more alarming symptoms of the 'culture of death', which is advancing above all in prosperous societies marked by an attitude of excessive preoccupation with efficiency and which sees the growing number of elderly and disabled people as intolerable and too burdensome."[2] This culture of death does not recognize our 4 Principles of Life. The Church teaches us that "Those whose lives are diminished or weakened deserve special respect. Sick or handicapped persons should be helped to lead lives as normal as possible" (*CCC* 2276).

The rising cost of health care is scaring many into denying the old and disabled the care they deserve. Some are saying, "Why waste the money?" Moreover, patients are being led to believe that this is actually in their best interest. "Whatever its motives and means, direct euthanasia consists in putting an end to the lives of handicapped, sick, or dying persons. It is morally unacceptable.

"Thus an act or omission which, of itself or by intention, causes death in order to eliminate suffering constitutes a murder gravely contrary to the dignity of the human person and to the respect due to the living God, his Creator. The error of judgment into which one can fall in good faith does not change the nature of this murderous act, which must always be forbidden and excluded" (*CCC* 2277).

History repeats itself

Many would be surprised to discover that the Nazi Party of World War II Germany began its murderous campaign by targeting the old and the disabled first. Using many of the same slogans we hear today, they killed people for their own good. Slogans are very dangerous, because they engage our emotions without engaging our intellect. They manipulate public opinion rather than informing it.

Once Germany began killing some people, it became easier to kill others. An interviewer once asked a Mafia hit man, "How can you bring yourself to kill another human being?" The hit man replied, "The first time was hard, but after that it was easy." What is true for a hit man can be true for a country. If a country is no longer ruled by just laws, it becomes ruled by men. In such an environment might makes right. Therefore the strongest and richest are able to impose their will on the rest. We then live according to the law of the jungle where only the strong survive.

Can you think of any examples of God's laws being ignored in our country? Can you think of any slogans being used to manipulate opinions about human life? Do news reports contribute to this confusion? Generally speaking, are the news media respectful of God's laws? Many times newspersons have strong opinions on the news they report. Can you think how their views can be expressed through their choice of words or tone of voice? What effect can this have on the opinions of viewers? Is this fair?

Josef Goebbels was the chief of Nazi Propaganda. His first project was titled the Merciful Release, which popularized the idea of a "life not worthy to be lived." This program entailed giving lethal injections to the elderly and the infirm. Up until that time suicide had been illegal. The program was considered a "great privilege" when it was introduced. It was such a privilege that Jewish citizens and other politically incorrect folks weren't eligible for it. That is, not initially.

An opportunity to love
Societies like these have their priorities backwards. People should always come first. Remember the 4 Principles of Life? Economic value and pleasure are only small elements of a person's total worth. They are far outweighed by being a child of God.

Moreover, the old and disabled can be of great value to those around them. Not for their economic output, but for the love they can produce. If we are open to it, they can increase our capacity to love because they are so in need of our attention. This is of far more value than money because love is eternal.

Caring for the old and disabled is an opportunity to grow in self-giving love, because there is no way they could ever repay us. Families caring for physically or mentally challenged members almost always say the experience made them better people. Why do you think this is so? Can you think of some examples?

The beginning of wisdom
God gave us life and he has given it to us forever. We should be afraid of nothing except abandoning him. "What will separate us from the love of Christ? Will anguish, or distress, or persecution, or famine, or nakedness, or peril, or the sword?" (Rom 8:35). That is why the beginning of wisdom is fear of the Lord (Prv 1:7). We should not let anything frighten us away from Him and doing things his way. The question: "What would Jesus do?" is the beginning of a good decision. No matter how scared we are, we should listen to Jesus before anyone else.

Do you remember the time Jesus fell asleep in the boat as he and his disciples were crossing the sea? You will recall that a great storm arose. One so fierce his disciples feared for their lives. After struggling their best, they eventually awoke Jesus saying, "Lord, save us! We are perishing!" He said to them, "Why are you terrified, O you of little faith?" (Mt 8:25-26).

Never forget "that all things work for good for those who love God, who are called according to his purpose" (Rom 8:28). Life is filled with perils. If we resist the temptation to cheat because we are afraid, we will survive the storms that come our way. With Jesus at our side we can overcome every obstacle, especially those involving his precious little ones.

Questions

1. What does it mean to rationalize our behavior?
   To rationalize our behavior is to compare ourselves to a standard other than God's.

2. How does fear cause evil? Give some examples.
   Fear causes us to lose our trust in God. Instead of seeking his will, we panic and take matters into our own hands. Recent history has shown how the hoax of overpopulation scared people into accepting contraception and abortion; now fear of rising health care costs is moving us towards euthanasia.

3. Why is knowing good from evil not enough?
   Simply knowing good from evil is not enough. We must also want to do what is good and avoid what is evil.

4. Why are the unborn, the aged and disabled a treasure?
   Meeting the needs of the unborn, the aged, and the disabled helps us to grow in self-giving love.

Notes

[1] *Humanae Vitae,* 17.
[2] *Gospel of Life,* 64.

CHAPTER 13

Life Is Hard

Suffering is a normal part of life

Suffering is not the worst thing that can happen to us. Sin is. While it is never desired, suffering is not to be avoided at all costs. It is a big part of life. In sports, the greater the suffering, the more valuable the victory. Heroism in the face of suffering makes the best stories. Have you ever tired of hearing an older person tell you the same stories over and over again? Can you remember what they were about? More than likely they involved suffering. They repeat the stories because they mean so much to them.

Similarly, friendships and marriages are strengthened through hardships borne together. Have you ever been through a difficult time and experienced someone remaining at your side through it all? If you have, you have found a true friend.

The value of suffering

Overcoming suffering is a defining moment for all of us. It is how we gain self-esteem and form our character. It makes us what we are today. If we let it, suffering can make us better people. However, many of us don't, because we respond to suffering in the wrong way. We ask God to change our situations, rather than asking for the help to change ourselves. Avoiding suffering is natural. But we should never forget that the real evil to avoid is sin, not suffering. No matter how we suffer for it, we should always try to do the right thing. Separating ourselves from God through sin only makes things worse.

How would you respond?

Take, for instance, euthanasia. Suppose an old person is admitted to the hospital, and you are given an opportunity to visit them. You can respond in two very different ways. One response may be: "What's the use of visiting? It is a waste of time. I am not a doctor. Either they will get better or they won't! Better that they die and reduce the surplus population." And so on, you get the idea. This is a self-centered approach to a difficult situation.

An other-centered response would think of the other person's feelings. You would recognize the medical hopelessness of the situation, but your evaluation is not based upon the probability of their resuming a productive life. Rather it is based on the 4 Principles of Life. The sick person is one who can know and love and be known and loved. Instead of abandoning them, we should visit them; sit and talk with them. If they are unable to talk, perhaps we could just hold their hand or brush their hair, anything that communicates our interest in them. In short, our response should be to help them bear their suffering and to suffer with them. This is the meaning of compassion.

We are too easy on ourselves

We are too quick to choose the efficient and pragmatic way. After living long lives of hard work and perhaps raising a family, is it right to cut them off? Instead of being fond of them, we try to hasten their deaths. We say, "It is better they die now with dignity, before they suffer any more." When the truth is that we want them to die before they cause *us* any more suffering. Euthanasia is not a good deed done for others; it is really done for ourselves. People don't choose to die (at least they don't when they are in their right minds). But they may feel like dying when they are unloved.

We may also suffer in sexual matters. Not giving in to our lust for sexual pleasure is difficult. Abstinence is a struggle. We have to fight against our rationalizations and excuses, "Everyone is doing it," "If I don't use it I'll lose it," etc. We are tempted to interpret "love" to mean physical love; giving in to our lust rather than waiting until marriage. This is how our popular culture encourages us to behave. Think about it. How often is marriage portrayed as something that should happen before sex?

Our challenge

Suffering to control our sexuality is not popular. It is considered by some to be "repressive"– even psychologically dangerous. They don't even think of it as possible (at least they don't want to because it means they would have to change). We have failed to realize that while self-expression is good, self-control is great. Chastity is the virtue of using our sexuality for good. For unmarried people this means abstinence, or remaining a virgin, and for married people it means being faithful to each other.

Some of our greatest saints were virgins. That is because men and women religious skip human marriage in this life. They make a solemn commitment called a vow of chastity whereby they abstain for their entire lives. In doing this they are able to give themselves totally to God, whereas married people give themselves to each other. Men and women religious are living signs to us that we are destined for communion with God. Their sacrifice also reminds us that we should avoid anything that separates us from Him. Even if we have to suffer for it.

Many of us are also afraid of babies, or at least of what they can do to our lives. That is why contraception and abortion are so prevalent. Babies are very demanding. They change our lives forever, because our lives must revolve around them. Once we become parents we can't do all the things we used to do. We have new responsibilities. Parenthood involves lots of work, and also lots of worry.

Suffering for the right reasons

When we love we also suffer. This is especially true regarding our children. We worry about their health, their friends, and their relationship with God. The list is endless. We want to protect them, but we can't live their lives for them. They are their own persons, and not our property. They have their own relationship with God; he is a father, not a grandfather.

Growing in virtue involves suffering. Our natural inclination is to be self-centered, but virtue demands that we think of higher things. It is a sacrifice because we sometimes have to say "no" to our selfishness in order to say "yes" to what is right. But it is a good kind of pain, like sore muscles after a good workout.

Suffering for the wrong reasons

But there is a kind of suffering that is never good. Sin is often its own punishment. For example, jealousy causes us pain when others possess more. It is not that we are in need of anything, it is simply the idea that others have more than we do. We would rather that everyone be poor than for anybody to be richer than us. Misery loves company. Possessions can also cause us great suffering if we are avaricious or greedy. We either live in fear of losing what we have, or fear that we don't have enough. Similarly, vanity causes us to suffer when we aren't appreciated as we would like; not being the center of attention can ruin our entire day.

Self-pity intensifies our sufferings beyond the normal. Have you ever met someone who always seems to suffer more than anyone else? No matter how bad anybody's situation is, they believe theirs is always worse. Another sort of self-inflicted suffering comes from being overly sensitive. Through this we imagine slights and insults when none are intended. We think we are being mistreated if someone uses the wrong tone of voice, or fails to say the right thing.

Perhaps the worst self-inflicted suffering of all is due to pride. We are all proud to a greater or lesser degree. It is the worst of our defects. It is sometimes called the sin of the Devil, because it was pride that caused the Devil to challenge God. Pride hates criticism. Criticism makes the proud person feel rejected, and as if the whole world was against them. Pride makes it difficult for us to admit our defects and failures (even though we can see the defects of others very clearly). It is also difficult to say thank you, which is the opposite of Christian gratefulness. These sufferings are of our own making, and therefore completely avoidable.

The real world

The point of this chapter is that life is hard. Real suffering does exist. The sooner we realize that it is a normal part of life, the sooner we will be able to deal with it. "Beloved, do not be surprised that a trial by fire is occurring among you as if something strange were happening to you" (1 Pt 4:12). The first step in dealing with our situation is eliminating all of the self-inflicted suffering mentioned above. As always, the best way to change the world is to change ourselves.

We also have to avoid ideas that promise heaven on earth. It isn't going to happen. "The world we live in often seems very far from the one promised us by faith. Our experiences of evil and suffering, injustice, and death, seem to contradict the Good News; they can shake our faith and become a temptation against it" (CCC 164). Millions of people have lost their lives because of governments trying to create the "perfect world." Isn't it ironic that millions have died in order to rid the world of suffering? They are dead, and the suffering is still here.

The meaning of suffering

The only real answer to suffering comes to us through our faith. Suffering is not meaningless. We can join Jesus in his work of redemption, if we learn to unite our suffering with him on the cross. "We must turn to the witnesses of faith: to Abraham, who 'in hope...believed against hope,' to the virgin Mary, who, in 'her pilgrimage of faith,' walked into the 'night of faith' in sharing the darkness of her son's suffering and death; and to so many others: 'Therefore, since we are surrounded by so great a cloud of witnesses, let us also lay aside every weight, and sin which clings so closely, and let us run with perseverance the race that is set before us, looking to Jesus the pioneer and perfecter of our faith,'" (CCC 165).

Being close to God does not mean being free of pain or difficulties. He has only promised his peace and the strength to face up to them. Once we know this and accept suffering as a part of life, we can carry our cross and endure it.

Here is a list of some of the reasons why we suffer:[1]

- to produce patience
- to produce joy
- to produce maturity
- to produce righteousness
- to silence the devil
- to teach us
- to purify our lives
- to make us Christ-like
- to glorify God
- to prevent sin
- to make us confess sin
- to chasten us for sin
- to prove our sonship
- to reveal ourselves to us
- to help our prayer life
- to make us examples
- to qualify us as counselors
- to further our witness
- to make us conquerors
- to see God's nature
- to drive us closer to God
- to prepare us for ministry
- to provide us reward
- to prepare us for the kingdom
- to show God's sovereignty

Here is a list of some good ways to respond to suffering:

- Expect suffering
- Commit to God from the start
- Don't try to understand it all
- Realize others suffer
- Don't despise your suffering
- Patiently endure steadfastly
- Thank God for your suffering
- Don't try to become a martyr
- Don't suffer needlessly
- Weigh your suffering against the coming glory

Questions

1. Is suffering normal part of life?
   Yes, suffering is a normal part of life.

2. Is suffering the worst thing that can happen to us?
   No, suffering is not the worst thing that can happen to us; falling into sin is much worse.

3. How can suffering be of value to us?
   Suffering can be of value to us if we let it change us for the better. We can pray for God's help in changing us, rather than asking him to change our difficult situation.

4. How can suffering be meaningful?
   Suffering can be meaningful since Jesus' suffering on the cross. We can join in his work of redemption by prayerfully uniting our suffering with his.

Notes

[1] *Willington's Book of Bible Lists.*

CHAPTER 14

Putting Ourselves In The Position To Win

We've got to play smart

Have you ever heard the curious phrase, "We beat ourselves"? It is really an excuse for losing to a weaker opponent. It is admitting that we blundered by not doing something we should have, or for doing something we should not have done. It means we didn't put ourselves in the best position to win. It is a variation of the old saying, "Life is hard, but it is harder when you are stupid." In other words, it means we did it to ourselves.

What are some of the ways to avoid "beating ourselves" in the pursuit of good relationships? As we discussed earlier, prayer, the sacraments, and forming our conscience are great ways to start. Time spent strengthening our intellect, will, and love is never wasted. This chapter will concern itself with other helpful advice.

Athletes and teams spend countless hours evaluating themselves. With this self-knowledge they are able to put themselves in good positions where the "odds are in their favor." When given the chance, they avoid situations where they are likely to fail. This makes sense, doesn't it? Everybody does it, at least when they are thinking and choosing carefully. Sure we take risks sometimes, but it is foolish to risk a lot, for a little. Would you bet a million dollars for the chance to win one? Of course you wouldn't. This reasoning can be applied to our relationships as well.

The opposite of smart is stupid

Many have taken risks with drugs and alcohol. They use them to "get in the mood" for socializing with others. It makes them less inhibited and more open, which is good up to a point. But it also weakens their wills and intellects, which makes them more susceptible to stupid ideas, which in turn become stupid actions.

Our natural shyness towards the opposite sex is a good thing. Modesty is a virtue that protects us from harm. It is a natural defense. This is not to say that we shouldn't have friends of the opposite sex, or that we shouldn't have a social life. But it does mean that we shouldn't ignore our instincts and sacrifice our higher goals for short-term popularity. It is interesting to note that drug, alcohol and even tobacco use is highest among the sexually active.

Decide what is important

This trade-off between popularity and good relationships is similar to the one faced by college football teams with different educational standards. One school gets more athletes because it doesn't require them to study hard, while the other school has higher academic standards, which disqualify many athletes who could otherwise help the team. Inevitably, when the team with the better athletes is winning, fans from the losing school begin chanting, "That's all right, that's okay, you will be working for us someday!" This sarcastic "congratulations" recognizes that although they lost a game, they'll win in the long run by keeping their academic standards high.

This is not to say that intelligence is the highest good. Being born with talent is not especially praiseworthy unless it is used for the good of others. However, it does illustrate that the longer something lasts, the more valuable it is. The body fades quicker than the mind, and they both fade quicker than the soul. Love is eternal. Loving is praiseworthy because it is something we choose, it is not something we are born with.

We may be All-Pro, a movie star, or the highest paid executive in the Fortune 500, but what good is that if Satan and all the devils are chanting, "That's alright, that's okay, you'll be living with us someday!"? Jesus said, "What profit would there be for one to gain the whole world and forfeit his life?" (Mt 16:26).

One thing leads to another

We don't intend to lose, but by intending to do those things that weaken us, we do. It is really the same thing; we put our selves in a losing position on purpose. Take dating, for example. There are things we can do to foster a good relationship, and there are things we can do that hurt our chances. Clearly, having a "study" date at home when our parents are away is a bad idea. The odds of success are against us. Did you know that this is when most kids become parents?

Whether we are on a study date or sitting in a car, the idea is the same. Avoid situations that will weaken our resolve to do what is right. Find good alternatives. Do something fun with a group of friends, or double date, etc. It takes a little forethought, but it is worth it. Don't expose yourself to difficult situations. Stay in control. A date should always fit our plans for the future. We shouldn't let others pressure us to live up to their expectations at the expense of our own. Besides, where will they be, years from now, when our dreams are gone?

Take a moment to think about your expectations and plans for the future. How could those plans change if you lost control? Next, make a list of dating alternatives that are fun, while avoiding the pitfalls we discussed. What would it take to make them happen?

Avoiding "the near occasions of sin" means avoiding environments or situations capable of getting us into trouble. Going to a party where drugs, alcohol, and sex are being abused is an example. Not preparing for an exam, and then sitting next to someone with an uncovered paper is another. But there are other, much more common situations to consider. Since such a large part of our time is devoted to entertainment, we are fooling ourselves if we think it too doesn't influence us.

The significance of entertainment

At the very least, bad entertainment weakens our resolve. By making bad behavior more familiar to us, we lose our ability to be shocked or repelled by it. It also gives us bad example. If people can influence us, than why can't the media do the same? If we look at pictures of immodestly dressed people, read steamy romance novels, or listen to raunchy music, we won't be thinking of the higher things. We must realize this when we choose our entertainment. If we adopt the attitude, "C'mon, tempt me some more!," we have already lost.

The media has a powerful influence over our imagination. This is important because, our thoughts control our actions. As they say, "junk in, junk out." We may not actually act it all out, but ingesting so much garbage can make us sick. Moreover, our choices in entertainment say a lot about us as a person. They are an indication of our intelligence and strength. They are an indication of how gullible we are in allowing ourselves to be seduced. Seduction is defined as the leading or drawing away from faith and principles, especially with regards to sexuality.

Take a moment and think of some popular forms of entertainment. How do they treat sexual relationships and marriage? Next, try to recall your moods and thoughts afterwards. Were they seductive? Were you weaker or stronger after exposing yourself to it? Be honest.

Another reason to avoid immoral entertainment is that in many cases it promotes the victimization of women and children. For some people, enslaving others for immoral purposes is a business. If we are willing to pay for it as consumers, they will exploit others in order to make money. For us it is a cheap thrill, but for someone else it may be a living hell.

Avoid mental mistakes
Which brings us to our final point. The biggest cause of beating ourselves is "mental mistakes." Any coach can tell you that mental mistakes kill your chances for success. We simply cannot make the mistake of believing that sex can be separated from marriage and procreation. For a sexual relationship to be true, beautiful and good all of these must be present.

This entire book underscores the consequences of separating them. It is a fundamental mistake. It causes: the lowering of morality, emotional and spiritual damage, the degradation of women and children, divorce, disease, death, government control of family life, and the treating of our bodies as if they were machines. And there is probably more yet to come if our genetic engineers fail to live by the 4 Principles of Life.

Our mistake is trying to control what we must never control, and not controlling what we must control. If sexuality is uncontrollable, then contraception, abortion and all of the aforementioned horrors are necessary. May it never be. If we follow God's plan, they are never necessary. Sexual urges can be controlled.

Separating procreation from married sexual love is at the heart of what John Paul II calls the Culture of Death. This culture believes that procreation needs to be artificially controlled, because we are not capable of controlling our sexuality. Whereas in the Culture of Life, sexuality is self-controlled, and the beginning of life is controlled by God. Where do you live? Would you rather control yourself and be in the hands of a merciful God, or be out-of-control and in the hands of the so-called "experts"?

Let's use our intellects and wills to choose wisely. Let's not merely pursue immediate gratification like the animals do. The Lord says, "I will instruct you and show you the way you should walk; I will counsel you, keeping my eye on you. Do not be senseless like horses or mules: with bit and bridle their temper must be curbed, else they will not come near you" (Ps 32:8-9). Let's not beat ourselves. Life is hard enough without being stupid.

Questions

1. Why is our natural shyness and modesty good?

   Our natural shyness and modesty is good because it protects us from sexual temptation and from tempting others. It is a natural defense that should be protected and not despised.

2. Is putting ourselves in weak positions bad even if we don't intend to do anything wrong?

   It is foolish and irresponsible to put ourselves in a weak position even if we don't intend to do anything wrong. If we intend to do what causes us to lose control, then we are responsible for the outcome.

3. Why is our choice of entertainment important?

   Entertainment can have a powerful influence on our imagination; it can inspire us to higher things or it can tempt us to sin. Since it is freely chosen, it says a lot about us as a person.

4. What is seduction?

   Seduction is the leading or drawing away from faith and principles, especially with regards to sexuality. Therefore if our faith and principles are true and good, seduction is an evil to be avoided.

5. Why is it important that we control our sexuality?

   It is important that we control our sexuality. Otherwise others will control it for us through contraception, abortion, and any number of other destructive means. Either we control ourselves and put ourselves in the hands of a merciful God, or we can be out-of-control and in the hands of the so-called "experts."

CHAPTER 15

It Is Not Over Until It Is Over

Where do you live?

Many people left Jesus because his teaching was too demanding. When Jesus asked the apostles if they too were leaving, St. Peter responded, "Master, to whom shall we go? You have the words of eternal life" (Jn 6:68). This curriculum is also demanding. And, like Peter, we should realize that there is no better alternative. This judgment is not just based on faith, it's also based on common sense and the lessons learned from the mistakes of others.

Life is so much easier when we know who we are, what we want, and where we are going. That is why this entire curriculum is based on the question: "Where do you live?" Unless we know where we live, we can easily be misled or demoralized. That is why it is important to resolve these questions as soon as we are able.

Be committed

Life Athletes is a coalition of over 200 professional and Olympic athletes who teach and inspire others to live lives of virtue, abstinence and respect for life. They invite others to join them in making the Life Athletes Commitment. Members believe that the Life Athletes Commitment gives them best shot at being happy in the long run. It upholds the 4 Principles of Life and strengthens them against the seduction of evil.

THE LIFE ATHLETES COMMITMENT
1. I will try to do what is right, even when it is difficult.
2. I will give myself only to that special person that I marry as my partner for life.
3. I will respect the lives of others, especially the unborn and the aged.
4. I will not quit or make excuses when I fail. I will try again.

Life is beautiful
Please don't look at this commitment as a set of rules meant to make life more difficult. If you do, think again. Use your imagination and reconsider the importance of life, and the greatness of our calling as sons and daughters of God. Good relationships free us to be the people we are made to be. They allow us to know and love others with grace and beauty. They allow us to act with confidence and power.

Just like athletes who spend hours training to express themselves in their sport, we can train ourselves in self-giving love. This will result in good friends, and the joy of knowing who we are and what we are all about. After all, it is only after learning their steps that dancers are able to express themselves fully. The same is true for us.

Talent and heart
We are all made up of two things: talent and heart. Our talent is God given. We are born with it. We cannot do anything to change it. Our hearts, on the other hand, we create through the choices we make in life. We might not have a Michael Jordan-sized talent, but we can have a Michael Jordan-sized heart, or bigger. The quality of our character is up to us. Life Athletes is a fellowship of the heart. Therefore anyone who makes the commitment is a member.

Winners and losers
In making the Life Athletes Commitment you are saying what *you* are going to do, not what others should be doing. You are also not saying that you were perfect in the past. Nobody is perfect. But that doesn't mean you should ever stop trying. The difference between winners and losers is that winners get up after they fall. Once you are down, you do not have to stay down. A famous foot-

ball coach, Vince Lombardi, once said, "Winning isn't everything; the *will* to win is everything." As long as we will try to do what is right, we are on the right road.

Staying in shape

And when you fall, you should go to confession for help. "The whole power of the Sacrament of Penance consists in restoring us to God's grace and joining us with him in an intimate friendship" (*CCC* 1468). There is nothing to be embarrassed about; going to confession is a healthy sign. It keeps us spiritually fit.

We are all sinners whether we admit it or not. In fact, God is happy when we do admit it. As Jesus said in telling the parable of the Prodigal Son, "But now we must celebrate and rejoice, because your brother was dead and has come to life again; he was lost and has been found" (Lk 15:32). When was the last time you went to confession? What are some of the reasons people give for not going to confession? Are these good reasons?

Keep your eyes on the prize

Whatever activities you decide to undertake, remember that building a culture of life is about relationships. It is the presence of Jesus in each soul, and also in every relationship. This is the unity that God wishes to establish in the world through his Church. It is also a foretaste of heaven. "Heaven is neither an abstraction nor a physical place in the clouds, but a living and personal relationship of union with the Holy Trinity."[1]

The invisible war

We are in a war with unseen forces trying to weaken our commitment, and to eventually ruin us. St. Paul tells us that "our struggle is not with flesh and blood, but with the principalities, with the powers, with the world rulers of this present darkness, with the evil spirits in the heavens" (Eph 6:12). These evil spirits are the fallen angels that rebelled against God.

St. John describes this rebellion, "The war broke out in heaven; Michael and his angels battled against the dragon. The dragon and its angels fought back, but they did not prevail and there was no longer any place for them in heaven. The huge dragon, the ancient serpent, who is called the Devil and Satan, who deceived the whole world, was thrown down to earth, and its angels were thrown down with it" (Rev 12:7-9). That is why St. Peter warns us, "Be sober and vigilant. Your opponent the devil is prowling around like a roaring lion looking for someone to devour" (1 Pet 5:8).

Knowledge of this spiritual conflict is helpful for a couple of reasons. First of all, if we don't know we are in a war, we are probably losing. Second, it helps us to understand our times, and to live accordingly. Satan's rebellion is the root cause of the Culture of Death. His proud boast, "I will be like God" started it all. Adam and Eve succumbed to the same temptation in the Garden of Eden when Satan promised them "you will be like gods" (Gen 3:5). Today, many of us fall for the same temptation when we decide for ourselves what is right and wrong, rather than following what God says.

As Satan succeeded in winning a third of the angels to his side, the Culture of Life found its champion in the Archangel Michael who responded with a declaration of his own. "Who is like God?" he said, thereby drawing the battle lines that exist to this day.

Contrary to popular belief, angels are not those cute and harmless little cherubs we see depicted in home and garden decorations. They are the "mighty ones who do his word" (*CCC* 329, Ps 103:20). Angels are immortal servants and messengers of God who are spirits possessing both an intellect and a will, and who are more perfect than any visible creature (*CCC* 330). The *Catechism of the Catholic Church* tells us, "Beside each believer stands an angel protector and shepherd leading him to life" (*CCC* 336). Many saints have developed a friendship with their Guardian Angels, and so can we.

Of all of these mighty spirits, the Church gives the Archangel Michael the highest place, for she refers to him as "Prince of the heavenly hosts." In Scripture, St. Michael appears as the head of God's armies: a champion of God's people in the Old Testament, and a mighty guardian in the New. St. Michael's example and intercession are powerful aids. "If Satan tries to induce us to sin, and promises honors, riches, happiness on conditions that we omit a good work, or commit an evil deed, let us ever oppose the tempter with the energetic words: Who is like unto God?"[2]

Do not be deceived. If we abandon God's authority, another authority will replace it, and it will not be our own. There are two alternatives: God the lover and author of life, or Satan the liar, thief and murderer. Who are you going to serve? If we choose God he will give us the help we need to resist evil influences. Spiritual battle requires spiritual weapons: prayer, the sacraments, and the intercession of the angels and saints – especially that of St. Michael.

Prayer to St. Michael
St. Michael, the Archangel, defend us in battle; be our safeguard against the wickedness and snares of the devil. May God rebuke him, we humbly pray, and do thou, Prince of the heavenly host, by the power of God thrust down to hell Satan and all the evil spirits, who wander through the world seeking the ruin of souls. Amen. [3]

Never give up. Never, never, never give up.
We must never give up hope. No matter what we have done we should never despair. As long as we have life in us, we can change. This requires an act of our will, and nobody can take away our will. God gave it to us, and not even the devil can take it away. However, he does have other methods. One of the devil's favorite temptations is to make us think we are no good, and that we will never be any good. He tricks people into hating their life and eventually into destroying themselves.

Even though the truth can sometimes hurt, ignoring the truth only makes a problem worse. It allows us to remain hard-hearted, and fails to warn others who are in danger. We all need special attention from time to time, and we should help those suffering from bad choices with a kind word, or by directing them to organizations and professionals that can help them.

Surprise ending
Have you ever set out on a long search only to discover that what you were looking for was right in front of you all the time? The two greatest commandments: "You shall love your God with all your heart, and with all your soul, and with all your mind," and "You shall love your neighbor as yourself," are things we have heard, but

often take for granted. After years of searching we can return to
where we began and realize that these are not only commandments,
but also the key to our happiness.[5]

Pope John Paul II concluded the *Gospel of Life* with this meditation
of hope, "The one who accepted 'Life' in the name of all for the
sake of all was Mary, the Virgin Mother; she is thus the most closely
and personally associated with the Gospel of Life. Mary's consent at
the Annunciation and her motherhood stand at the very beginning
of the mystery of life which Christ came to bestow on humanity.
Through her acceptance and loving care for the life of the Incarnate
Word, human life has been rescued from condemnation to final and
eternal death.[5]

"We look to her who is for us 'a sign of sure hope and solace.'

O Mary,
Bright dawn of the new world,
Mother of the living,
To you do we entrust the cause of life:
Look down, O Mother,
Upon the vast numbers
Of babies not allowed to be born,
Of the poor whose lives are made difficult,
Of men and women
Who are victims of brutal violence,
Of the elderly and the sick killed
By indifference or out of misguided mercy.
Grant that all who believe in your Son
May proclaim the Gospel of Life
With honesty and love
to the people of our time.
Obtain for them the grace
To accept that Gospel
As a gift ever new,
The joy of celebrating it with gratitude
Throughout their lives
And the courage to bear witness to it
Resolutely, in order to build,
Together with all people of good will,
The civilization of truth and love,

To the praise and glory of God,
The Creator and lover of life."[6]

Questions

1. What is spiritual warfare?

   It is recognizing the spiritual dimension of our struggle in this life, and using the means God gives us to overcome our adversary, the Devil. Such means include: prayer, the sacraments, and the intercession of the angels and saints – especially St. Michael the Archangel.

2. What is the difference between talent and heart?

   The difference between talent and heart is that our talent is God given, we are born with it; we have nothing to do with it. Our hearts are quite a different matter. We make our hearts through the choices we make in life; we are what we choose.

3. What is the difference between winners and losers?

   The difference between winners and losers is that winners try again after they lose. Very few winners have never lost, and they never would have won if they had given up after they lost.

4. Why is Mary such an important figure in the Gospel of Life?

   Mary is an important figure in the Gospel of Life, because by her acceptance and loving care for Jesus she made it possible for all people to be rescued from final condemnation and eternal death.

5. What is Heaven?

   Heaven is neither an abstraction nor a physical place in the clouds, but a living and personal relationship of union with the Holy Trinity.

6. What is the purpose of the Sacrament of Penance?

   The whole power of the Sacrament of Penance consists in restoring us to God's grace and joining us with him in an intimate friendship (*CCC* 1468).

Notes
[1] John Paul II, General Audience July 21, 1999.
[2] *St. Michael and the Angels,* p. 72.
[3] Promulgated by Pope Leo XIII.
[4] Matthew 22:36-39.
[5] *Gospel of Life,* 102.
[6] *Ibid.,* 105.

Additional copies may be obtained through
Life Athletes
410 Plaza Building
210 South Michigan Street
South Bend, IN 46601

www.lifeathletes.org